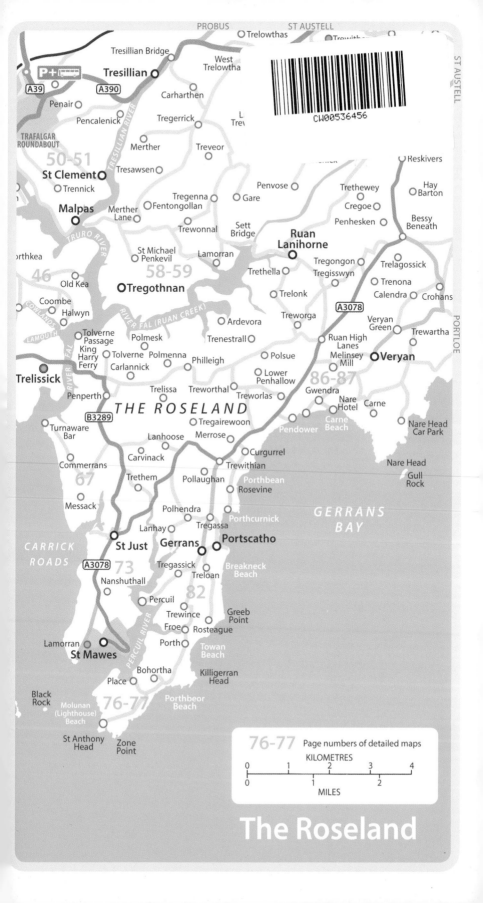

The Roseland

PROBUS   ST AUSTELL

ST AUSTELL

Trelowthas

Trowith—

Tresillian Bridge

West Trelowtha

Tresillian

P+ 🚌

A39   A390

Carharthen

Penair

Tregerrick

L Trev

Pencalenick

Treveor

TRAFALGAR ROUNDABOUT

Merther

Tresawsen

50-51

St Clement

Penvose

Trethewey

Hay Barton

Reskivers

Trennick

Tregenna

Gare

Cregoe

Bessy Beneath

Fentongollan

Malpas

Merther Lane

Penhesken

TRURO RIVER

Trewonnal

Sett Bridge

Ruan Lanihorne

orthkea

St Michael Penkevil

Lamorran

Tregongon

Trelagossick

46

Old Kea

58-59

Trethella

Tregisswyn

Trenona

Coombe

Tregothnan

Trelonk

Calendra

Crohans

Halwyn

RIVER FAL (RUAN CREEK)

Ardevora

Treworga

A3078

Veryan Green

Trewartha

COOMBE

Tolverne Passage

Polmesk

Trenestrall

Ruan High Lanes

LAMOUTH

King Harry Ferry

Tolverne

Polmenna

Philleigh

Polsue

Melinsey Mill

Veryan

Carlannick

Lower Penhallow

86-87

Trelissick

Penperth

Trelissa

Treworthal

Treworlas

Gwendra

Nare Hotel

Carne

THE ROSELAND

Pendower

Carne Beach

B3289

Tregairewoon

Nare Head Car Park

Turnaware Bar

Lanhoose

Merrose

Carvinack

Curgurrel

Nare Head

Commerrans

Trewithian

Gull Rock

67

Trethem

Pollaughan

Porthbean

GERRANS BAY

Messack

Rosevine

Polhendra

Porthcurnick

Lanhay

Tregassa

St Just

Gerrans

Portscatho

CARRICK ROADS

A3078

73

Tregassick

Breakneck Beach

Nanshuthall

Treloan

82

Percuil

Trewince

Greeb Point

PERCUIL RIVER

Froe

Rosteague

Lamorran

Porth

St Mawes

Towan Beach

Bohortha

Killigerran Head

Place

Black Rock

Porthbeor Beach

Molunan (Lighthouse) Beach

76-77

St Anthony Head

Zone Point

76-77   Page numbers of detailed maps

KILOMETRES

0   1   2   3   4

0   1   2

MILES

South Cornwall

Falmouth and Roseland

Truro, St Mawes, Portscatho, Trelissick

By Neil Reid

EXPLORING CORNWALL AND SCILLY

No.5

Credits, acknowledgements and further reading

The following books and websites provided much of the information
in this guidebook and are a good place to start for those who
would like to gain a more detailed picture of this area and its history.

Cornwall Historic Environment Record
Geology of Britain Viewer at the British Geological Survey website
Cornish Archaeology Annual reports of the Cornwall Archaeological Society
Folklore of Cornwall Tony Deane and Tony Shaw, The History Press (2003)
Fortress Falmouth: A conservation plan for the historic defences of Falmouth
Vol 1 & 2, Richard Linzey, English Heritage (2000)
Fal Estuary Historic Audit Jeanette Ratcliffe, Cornwall Archaeological Unit, Cornwall Council (1997)
Cornwall's Geology and Scenery: an introduction Colin M Bristow, Cornish Hillside Publications (1996)
Cornish Place-name Elements OJ Padel, English Place-name Society Vol LVI/LVII (1985)
Prehistoric Cornwall John Barnatt, Turnstone Press Limited (1982)
Cornish Shipwrecks, The South Coast Richard Larn and Clive Carter, David & Charles (1971)
The Saints of Cornwall, Part Three: Saints of the Fal and its Neighbourhood
Gilbert H Doble, Llanerch Press (1998)

Portrait of Edward Boscawen on page 56 by Sir Joshua Reynolds
Painted circa 1750–1760 © National Maritime Museum,
Greenwich, London, Greenwich Hospital Collection
Watercolour illustrations: Bridgitte Livesley

First published in 1995 as *The Map and Guide to Exploring the River Fal and Roseland*
This edition © Neil Reid and Friendly Guides 2019
Contains OS data © Crown copyright and database right (2019)

ISBN 978-1-904645-51-1 (Paperback)
5th Edition
No.5 in the *Exploring Cornwall and Scilly* series

The Friendly Guides logo is a trademark of the Reid Partnership
1 St Mary's Terrace, Penzance, Cornwall, TR18 4DZ
Tel: 01736 369194 Email: sales@friendly-guides.uk
www.friendly-guides.uk

Contents

Introduction
One foot forever in the sea

Cowlands Creek near Roundwood Quay

IT'S A SURPRISE TO COME ACROSS A TIDAL ESTUARY AT ALL, so deep in the heart of rural Cornwall; to be walking through a landscape of fields and country lanes far from the sea, but then to stumble upon a valley brimful of seawater. However, even on its furthest reaches more than sixteen kilometres from the coast, the Fal Estuary remains unmistakably a feature of the sea, governed by its rhythms and personality. When the tide falls on the upper reaches, the tiny size of the freshwater streams that feed the estuary are revealed, so insignificant they're often lost out of sight between the mud banks. These small streams could never have carved out the deep river valleys we see today. For that we need to look back to more turbulent climatic times. In the last million years alone there have been as many as ten glacial periods – times when Cornwall was locked into brutal cycles of freezing and thawing. In the coldest periods (and the last glacial period only ended about 10,000 years ago), sea level was as much as 100 metres lower than today as huge volumes of water were locked up in ice sheets. It was probably torrents of seasonal meltwater in these glacial periods that did the most to cut the deep valleys of the Fal Estuary. We now live in a much warmer period and sea levels are correspondingly higher. As a result, the sea now flows far inland, submerging the old river valleys and transforming them into sea creeks. When the tide retreats on the upper reaches of the estuary, at least for a few hours, they are reclaimed for the land and take on a pensive mood broken only by the cries of curlew and redshank busily feeding on the mud flats before the tide floods inland once more.

The atmosphere of the estuary and creeks

One of the great pleasures of exploring the Fal Estuary is seeing how land and sea interact in different ways, in different parts of the estuary. On the upper reaches near **Tresillian**, **Truro** and **Ruan Lanihorne**, the daily ebb and flow of the tide animates the landscape and markedly changes the mood and atmosphere. At low water when they dry out, these creeks can feel abandoned and forlorn, and the whole landscape seems to hold its breath, waiting for the tide to return (page 61). When it does, it steals in quietly like an interloper to inundate mud banks and salt marsh, flooding the broad valleys to create an improbable inland sea. **Ruan Creek** is the archetypal example of the estuary on its upper reaches; undisturbed by the outside world, its peaceful mood is favoured by shy river birds that congregate here to feed on the mud banks exposed by the falling tide (photo page 61).

Between **Malpas** and **Turnaware Bar** on the middle reaches of the estuary (which remain navigable even at low water), the broad valleys that are such a feature of the upper reaches are replaced by taller, steeper banks cut by the combined force of the Fal, Truro and Tresillian rivers. The high wooded banks tower over the water blocking out everyday noises, but, oddly, despite the many twists and turns in the creeks, sounds on the water can be strangely amplified and carry long distances. Even the sound of a small outboard engine can reverberate far along the water, making it difficult to work out if it's just round the corner, or in some far away creek. Deprived of the usual cues, your senses are thrown slightly off-balance (like in a snowy landscape) adding to the dreamy mood. The side creeks around **Trelissick**, **Roundwood** and **Coombe** retain something of the atmosphere of the upper reaches, but they never feel so completely abandoned by the falling tide or so engulfed by the melancholy mood found there. Cowlands and Lamouth creeks are some of the most beautiful places in this book (photo opposite).

Below **Turnaware Bar** the river, released from the constriction of its middle reaches, opens out into **Carrick Roads**. Two small side creeks join at Mylor and St Just. Their short courses travel little more than a kilometre inland. **Restronguet Creek** and the **Percuil River** have longer courses and they illustrate, in miniature, the transitional stages seen on the estuary as a whole: abandoned mudflats on the upper reaches at low water, narrow navigable middle reaches and the broad lower reaches. The **Percuil River** is particularly beautiful, exhibiting throughout its short course the most harmonious balance between land and sea on the whole estuary.

Looking over the entrance of Carrick Roads towards St Anthony Lighthouse and the Roseland

The estuary as a highway

The many creeks and inlets on the estuary present a considerable obstacle to overland travel, and for most of human history, the estuary itself has been the easiest and most convenient way to get around. The first people to arrive in any numbers along this natural highway were hunters and gatherers moving north from Europe into a thawing landscape at the end of the last glacial period, about 10,000 years ago. Except for the odd flint arrowhead or scrapper that occasionally turns up in a ploughed field, little physical evidence of their lives remain, and many of their coastal camps must now be lost to the sea which, at that time, was rapidly rising as the climate warmed.

The first concerted attempt to parcel out and cultivate the landscape began in the late Stone Age (4000–2300BC) and really got into its stride in the Bronze Age (2300–800BC). Again, few physical structures survive from that time as more than two thousand years of ploughing has done much to erase their fields, buildings and monuments, which exist now only as shadows, showing up as crop marks on aerial pictures. Some monuments are remembered in place names so, for instance, the Cornish word element *cruc* for *barrow* or *burial mound* occurs around the estuary in place names like Polcreek and Creek Stephen. We can be fairly confident that, although no obvious structure is visible, this was the site of a prehistoric burial mound. Of the Bronze Age monuments that have survived, the barrow or burial mound at **Carne Beacon** is perhaps the most prominent along with the standing stones at **Mylor** and **St Clement** churches.

By the Iron Age (800BC–AD43) much of the landscape we see today was already in place, with a mosaic of dispersed farmsteads on the best soils, areas of heathland on the higher ground and thick oak woods on the river banks. These farmers gathered at ramparted enclosures like **Roundwood Fort**, **Veryan Castle** and **Dingerein Castle** to meet, trade and celebrate ritual. Most of these sites remained in use well into the Dark Ages (AD410–1066) and they still stand out clearly in the landscape. The origins of the waterside churches on the estuary also go back to the early Dark Ages. Celtic missionaries, travelling between Brittany, Wales and Ireland in the 5th and 6th centuries, set up holy enclosures or *lanns* (as in Ruan *Lan*-ihorne and *Lan*-morran) on the water's edge where they landed. The churches we see today date from the 13th to 15th centuries, but their sites would have originated in the Dark Ages as simple oval enclosures, perhaps with a stone cross to gather around for prayer. The crosses were sometimes reworked prehistoric stones like the **Ignioc Stone** at **St Clement** and a similar giant at **Mylor Church**. Many missionaries became venerated as saints of the Celtic Church, and their names are found all around the estuary – Mylor, Feock, Kea, Ruan, Fili, Mawes.

In more recent centuries, trade and commerce was carried out on ships, barges and working boats – each part of the river having a design suited to its conditions: flat-bottomed barges to carry cargo to the shallower parts of the estuary, the gaff-rigged oyster boats that still fish Carrick Roads today, or the sleek pilot cutters designed for getting out to home-bound ships as swiftly as possible. Almost every farm, estate and village had its own quay or landing beach to bring in coal and fertiliser and to export crops, stone and mineral ore to market. Most, of course, are little used now, but the quays at **Roundwood**, **Greatwood** and **Ruan Lanihorne** are interesting places to visit. The working boats and pilot cutters are raced in the season, and the Maritime Museum in Falmouth has more on their history.

For many people living around the estuary their work and life was completely focused on the water. The houses at Coombe, for instance, were not even connected to the public road network until the 1920s. The Kea plums that overhang **Cowlands Creek** used to be harvested directly into boats and taken to the quayside market in Truro, and well into the 20th century, beer was delivered to the Pandora Inn by boat because Passage Hill was too steep for the brewery drays. It was only in the 1950s that this waterborne trade moved to the roads. In recent years some of those lost connections have been reestablished, and you can explore most parts of the estuary by ferry and water taxi.

Admirals and explorers

The people who lived around the Fal Estuary would often spend as much time on the water as on the land, and were as at home on a heaving and pitching deck as on solid ground. The rivers and creeks have nurtured many famous seaman and adventurers, people like **Sir John Killigrew** (c.1520–1584), an Elizabethan buccaneer, part pirate, part national hero, second governor of Pendennis Castle and who helped to found the town of Falmouth. Many who grew up on the river joined the navy to fight and forge an empire. **Admiral 'Old Dreadnought' Boscawen** (1711–1761) of Tregothnan was rear admiral by the age of 36, and a scourge of the French fleet all his life. **Sir Richard Spry** (1715–1775) of Place near St Mawes, Commander of His Majesty's land and sea forces in America, envoy to the Emperor of Morocco and the States of the Barbary Coast, was captured and held to ransom by the Spanish in the West Indies. **Admiral Sir Barrington Reynolds** (1786–1861) went to sea aged ten, was wrecked, imprisoned, ransomed and released by the French, all by the time he was twelve. There are beautiful monuments to these men in the churches at St Clement, St Michael Penkevil and St Anthony at Place. They are some of the best art in Cornwall (photos page 52 and page 56).

At the top of Lemon Street in Truro is a monument to the Victorian explorer **Richard Lander** (1804–1834). He left Cornwall on a merchantman at the age of thirteen, and later became one of the first explorers of the heart of Africa. In 1830 he led an expedition to search for the source of the River Niger, for which he was awarded the first Royal Gold Medal of the Royal Geographical Society. His exploits and adventures, which included being captured and held ransom by tribesmen, were turned into a popular comic book serial. In 1834

a second expedition was sponsored by British businessmen with the object of opening up new markets in the area, and this time he was accompanied by a barge full of cowrie shells, the local currency of the Niger peoples. However, on this occasion his luck ran out and he was killed and later buried at Fernando Po. Such was the popular acclaim for this Victorian adventurer that a monument was quickly erected at the top of Lemon Street in Truro to commemorate his life.

Richard Lander

St Anthony Lighthouse

Exploring the estuary

A surprising amount of the western side of Carrick Roads (as far as Restronguet Passage) is accessible on foot just by taking the ferry from Falmouth to Flushing. Similarly, the 45 minute ferry trip to **Trelissick** from Falmouth or St Mawes will place you right in the heart of the middle reaches of the estuary. At Trelissick you might easily spend a day looking around the gallery, gardens and woods. Alternatively, you can take the option to walk to some of the more out-of-the-way places like Roundwood Quay, Old Kea and Coombe. Taking the ferry to **St Mawes** similarly opens up many possibilities for walks on the eastern side of the Carrick Roads. Following the water's edge will get you up to St Just, Messack Point and Turnaware Bar. A small seasonal ferry runs from St Mawes to Place opening up walks on the Percuil River and on the coast to St Anthony Head and Portscatho.

The more remote corners of the estuary – places like **Ruan Creek** – will have to be explored by car. These atmospheric corners are probably the least visited but are some of the loveliest places on the whole estuary. Simply deciding to visit the waterside churches and old ferry landing places like **Halwyn**, **Tolverne**, **Kea Woods**, **Restronguet Passage**, **Malpas Point** and **Percuil** will take you to some of the most hidden away places. But perhaps the best way to get a flavour of the estuary is to hire a kayak or motor boat from Falmouth, Mylor Harbour or Loe Beach. Once on the water you will feel the excitement and thrill of being part of the life of the river. Admiral 'Old Dreadnought' Boscawen would certainly have approved.

Ferry coming into the
Prince of Wales Pier in Falmouth

1. Falmouth and Carrick Roads

Open sea and blustery skies

W E START ON THE COAST JUST NORTH of the Helford Estuary at **Rosemullion Head** from where there are fine views over Falmouth Bay to Pendennis Castle and the Roseland. In fact, the walks around Mawnan and Rosemullion Head have many similarities to those around St Anthony Head on the Roseland – an attractive and rapidly changing mix of woodland, cliff and beach all condensed into a small area. The wide and sandy beach at **Maenporth** is the most popular family beach in the whole Falmouth area. In scale and setting, it is rather the exception to the normal pattern on this coast, which is usually for tiny, quartz-pebbled coves that attract families looking for a more out-of-the-way place to spend a sunny day. Of the smaller coves, the best are Porth Sawsen, Porthallack, Nansidwell and Bream Cove.

As the coast path heads north from Maenporth towards The Stack (Pennance Point), two small pebbly coves, Newporth Beach and Sunny Cove, can be found tucked under the cliffs. Both were favourite locations for the Impressionist painter Henry Scott Tuke (1858–1929). He's well known for his paintings of male nudes, often posed bathing or on a beach, including a portrait of TE Lawrence on Newporth Beach painted in 1921. Tuke lived and worked in a small cottage on the Swanpool side of The Stack, and his work is often on display at Falmouth Art Gallery.

The beaches at Gyllyngvase and Swanpool, and the attraction of the National Maritime Museum and Pendennis Castle make **Falmouth** the major focus for visitors on the estuary. It is also the hub of the ferry network, and most places are accessible from either Prince of Wales Pier or Custom House Quay. Regular year-round ferries run to St Mawes and Flushing. They are supplemented in the season by services to Trelissick Garden, Malpas, Truro and the Helford. The Maritime Museum has displays of small craft from

HIGHLIGHTS

PANDORA INN
Sitting on the pontoon under a starry sky.

ENYS HOUSE
Famed for its display of bluebells in the spring.

USEFUL FERRIES

Check the Fal River website for timetables, latest information and updates. Main ferry landing places are marked ⬤ on the maps. Other potential landing places are marked ◯.

❸ There's a frequent year-round ferry service between Flushing and the Prince of Wales Pier (PWP), Falmouth.
❹ A year-round foot ferry runs between PWP and St Mawes. Additional services leave from Custom House Quay (CHQ) in Falmouth in the season.
❻ A seasonal foot ferry runs from PWP and CHQ in Falmouth to Trelissick, Malpas (low water) and Truro (high water).
❼ Seasonal cruises to the Helford leave from PWP in Falmouth.
❽ Year-round sea safaris leave from Discovery Quay (DQ) near the National Maritime Museum in Falmouth.

Falmouth

all over the world, including Inuit kayaks and old steam boats, as well as interactive displays, a lookout tower and galleries that document Cornwall's connection to the sea. Pendennis Castle has seen more than 400 years of active service. There are displays around the site and in the main keep. Many emplacements have been refitted with guns, and there are popular battle reenactments and medieval tournaments in the summer. Don't miss the tunnel that takes you under the walls to the Half Moon Battery (page 25).

We then leave Falmouth and follow the western side of **Carrick Roads**, the great natural harbour that makes up the lower part of the Fal Estuary. In the summer it teems with dinghies, yachts and classic working boats. Amidst all this activity, ocean-going ships come and go to Falmouth Docks or are towed up to King Harry Reach near Trelissick for long-term storage. It's just a short ferry ride across the Penryn River from Falmouth to Flushing and the popular walks to **Mylor Harbour**. This is a base for the oyster boats that are such a handsome sight in the winter as they trawl back and forth in Carrick Roads (photo page

Pendennis Castle

32). The short valley that runs up from Mylor Creek ends at Enys House, famous for its bluebell meadows in the spring. The house, despite its lack of interior decoration and furniture, is the most beautiful on the estuary. From Mylor Bridge the old main road heads straight to the old ferry crossing at Restronguet Passage, the setting for the **Pandora Inn**. No trip to the Fal Estuary would be complete without an afternoon or evening spent sitting outside on the pontoon and enjoying a pint and a crab sandwich.

Maenporth, Penjerrick, Mawnan and Rosemullion Head

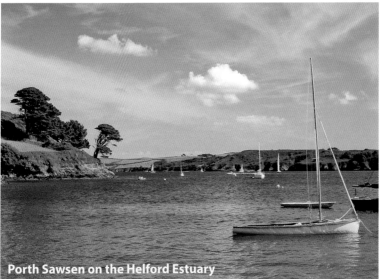

Porth Sawsen on the Helford Estuary

The Helford Estuary is a popular excursion south from Falmouth. The whole estuary and the famous subtropical gardens at Trebah and Glendurgan are covered in our *Helford Guidebook*, so in this book we start just north of the mouth of the Helford at **Mawnan Church** and **Rosemullion Head**. The coastline here is typical of south Cornwall – low slate cliffs dotted every few hundred metres by small, enchanting coves like **Porthallack**, **Porth Sawsen**, **Nansidwell** and **Bream Cove**. We then continue north along the coast to the family beach at **Maenporth** and on to the secret garden at **Penjerrick**.

Mawnan Church and Rosemullion Head

Mawnan Church stands close to the coast path and is a convenient starting point for the walks around Rosemullion Head. There are fine panoramic views from Rosemullion Head over Falmouth Bay to Pendennis Castle and the Roseland. The white outline of St Anthony Lighthouse clearly stands out and, in the distance beyond, you should be able to make out the shape of Nare Head (where this book ends). Further still, on a clear day, you'll see Dodman Point near Mevagissey. If you then turn southwards you are looking over the mouth of the Helford Estuary to Dennis Head and Nare Point with its Coastwatch Station. Just out to sea lies the infamous Manacles reef, which emerges as the tide falls. There are many small pebbly coves on this coast, any one of which makes a good place to stop, enjoy the view, picnic and swim. This walk can be easily extended into a longer hike to Maenporth returning to Mawnan Smith, and then descending through the beech woods of Carwinion Valley to the banks of the Helford.

BUDOCK WATER, FALMOUTH

FALMOUTH

FOOTPATH THE STAC

Penjerrick Garden

Tregedna Farm

Pennance Mill

Penrose Farm

Su (Art

Newporth Beach

Rosemerryn Farm

Newporth Head

Ben Asdale 1978 Remains visible on the rocks

Bareppa

P
Maenporth Beach

Carlidnack Round

High Cliff

CARLIDNACK ROAD

CARLIDNACK LANE

EXTENSION

MAENPORTH ROAD

Trelawne Hotel

Meudon Farm

Meudon

The Hutches

Mawnan Smith

Meudon Hotel

Bream Cove

Nansidwell (Woodlands) Beach

Red Lion

Chenhalls

P

Gatamala Cove

School

Sowan's Hole

World War II anti-aircraft gun battery (ruined)

Carwinion

Nansidwell Manor

Nansidwell Farm

Rosemullion Farm

Endevour

TREBAH AND GLENDURGAN GARDENS, HELFORD PASSAGE

OLD CHURCH ROAD

RECOMMENDED WALK

Rosemullion Head

Carwinion Valley

Trerose Farm

Prisk Cove

Mawnan

P

P

Mawnan Church

August Rock

Porth Sawsen or Cow Beach

Mawnan Shca

Parson's Beach

Shag Rock

Porthallack Beach

Mawnan Rock

Rock Island Bridge 1920

Toll Point

Toll Hole

The Gedges

HELFORD ESTUARY

Ponsence Cove (Grove Beach)

Maggie 1928

The Gew

Maenporth

Maenporth

This is a favourite beach of many Falmouth residents seeking refuge from the very busy beaches in the town. Its beautiful setting, in a deep inlet surrounded by fields, is only matched in this book by the beaches at Towan and Porthcurnick on the Roseland. The seasonal beach cafe provides water sports hire, and The Cove restaurant is just over the road. The car park at the back of the beach fills quickly in the summer and there are no real alternatives nearby, so plan to get here early.

Penjerrick Garden

The garden was laid out in the mid 19th century by Robert and Barclay Fox, part of the same family that laid out the gardens at Trebah, Glendurgan and Meudon. The family were shipping merchants in Falmouth and stocked their gardens with specimen plants brought back on ships from around the world. Penjerrick is less commercial and on a smaller scale than the gardens at Trebah and Glendurgan, being one of Cornwall's 'lost' gardens, hidden away and wild. It's full of spring and early summer flowering plants as well as ponds surrounded by tree ferns and bamboos. The garden is open on selected days, so check opening times before you travel.

Meudon, Bream Cove and Nansidwell (Woodlands) Beach

The house and gardens at Meudon Hotel were established by the Fox family. At the bottom of the Meudon's valley garden are two small shingle beaches that merge into one sandy cove as the tide falls – Bream Cove and Nansidwell (or Woodlands) Beach. As they are a fifteen minute walk from the road they are rarely crowded, but they are a popular choice for those looking for a more remote family beach. There is parking for about twenty cars on the roadside just before Chenhalls; however, this quickly fills on sunny days. The beaches are best visited as the tide turns and falls, so check tide times before you go. Once parked on the road, look out for a small tarmac track with a large metal farm gate and a concrete stile. Cross the stile and follow the path to the coast. Meals and cream teas are served at Meudon Hotel, and the garden is also open on selected days.

The path from Chenhalls to Nansidwell Beach

Parking, shorter walks and leisurely strolls

Parking can be tricky in this popular area. There is a beach car park at **Maenporth** but it fills quickly on sunny summer days. Visitors to **Nansidwell (Woodlands) Beach** will find space for about 20 cars on the roadside before **Chenhalls**. Look out for a metal farm gate and a concrete stile – this is the path down to the cove from the public road.

For walks around **Rosemullion Head** there is a little roadside parking just before **Mawnan Church** (under the trees just past the house called Well Meadow) and the church has a small car park. There is roadside parking in **Mawnan Smith** on the road to Helford Passage (Grove Hill).

A walk from Mawnan Church to Rosemullion Head, Nansidwell Beach and Carwinion Woods

*This small area has a great variety of scenery and views with lots of places to swim and picnic. There's a small car park at **Mawnan Church**. If it's full or there's a service on, there is a little roadside parking just before the church under the trees between **Well Meadow** and **Middle Trerose** (marked P on the map). Alternatively, park in **Mawnan Smith** or on the roadside near **Chenhalls**.*

Park at **Mawnan Church**. The path skirts the churchyard to the side of the lych gate under the trees. After about 30m, look for a path on the left to take you to the coast path (the main path from the car park continues to Porthallack). Turn left at the coast path; you are in the woods above **Parson's**

Beach (where you can swim off the rocks). As you leave the trees you should see **Prisk Cove** below you. The path falls gently to a stream and then rises again to the far end of the cove. Here you have the choice to keep on the coast to **Rosemullion Head** or to cut across the headland. The path is then clear to **Nansidwell (Woodlands) Beach**.

Turn inland just past the small stream and follow the path up to the public road at **Chenhalls**. At the road turn left past **Nansidwell Manor**. Turn down **Old Church Road** for a shortcut back to the church. Otherwise, keep right at the sharp corner and just 10m past **Carwinion Playing Field** leave the road and turn left down a track through **Carwinion Woods** to **Porth Sawsen**. Follow the coast path to **Porthallack**. The track back to the church starts inland above the beach.

Distance
Mawnan Church–Rosemullion Head–Nansidwell –Carwinion 6km (3¾ miles). Extension to Maenporth and Meudon Farm adds 2.5km (1½ miles) to the total.

Food and drink
Red Lion and Mawnan Stores in Mawnan Smith. Meudon Hotel for meals and afternoon tea. Beach Cafe at Maenporth.

Porthallack

Falmouth, Pendennis Castle and Carrick Roads

Looking over Little Dennis Blockhouse and Carrick Roads to the Roseland

Falmouth developed much later than most Cornish towns, and until the 16th century there was nothing more than a small fishing hamlet called Penny-come-quick close to where the Prince of Wales Pier stands today (from the Cornish *Pen y cum gwyk* or *head of the narrow valley*). At this time, the only other building of any importance in the area was the semi-fortified Elizabethan manor of Arwenack. It stands today opposite the Maritime Museum ringed by houses and terraces; then it was surrounded by open fields, a deer park and orchards. That Arwenack Manor was fortified is a clue to why a settlement hadn't developed here – it was just too open and exposed to the predations of pirates, privateers and warships to be a sensible site for a large settlement. Almost all of the older settlements around the estuary, like Penryn, Truro and Tregony, are tucked safely away at the head of creeks, almost out of sight from Carrick Roads.

The danger was not always one sided though, and Sir John Killigrew (c.1520–1584) of Arwenack Manor was himself a notorious rogue, fond of looting and plundering any foreign ship that took refuge in Carrick Roads. His wife Lady Killigrew was no different and was accused of involvement in the murder of a crew member on one raid, and although she was later pardoned by Queen Elizabeth I, there were suspicions of bribery and chicanery. The construction of Pendennis Castle in the 1540s helped to establish security and the rule of law (although its second governor was Sir John Killigrew), laying the foundation that allowed the town to prosper and develop along the waterfront between Penny-come-quick and Arwenack Manor.

Swanpool Beach

Truro and Penryn, seeing a potential threat to their own prosperity in this upstart town, set out to strangle the newcomer at birth, and that struggle provoked a rivalry that survives to this day. In the end it was Falmouth's support of the King in the English Civil War (1642–1651) that finally set the town on a course to dominate the estuary. The strong resistance by Royalist troops at Pendennis Castle was used as a lever to persuade Charles II, on his restoration in 1660, to grant a charter to Falmouth. Truro's traders and citizens had been sympathetic to the Parliamentarian cause, and granting Falmouth this privilege was a calculated snub to them. Crucially, Charles also gave Falmouth rights over shipping entering Carrick Roads and the revenue that flowed from it. When in 1688 the Royal Mail Packet Service was sited here, Falmouth became not only the major port on the estuary but also an international port. The packet ships were small, fast ships that carried mail to Portugal, the West Indies and America (see the exhibition in the Maritime Museum). In the end it was Penryn that lost out the most, finding itself marooned at the top of St Gluvius Creek while the docks and quays of Falmouth grew to dominate the river in the 18th and 19th centuries.

The older parts of town look to the estuary, and this is where the shops, docks, piers and quays are sited and where the National Maritime Museum was more recently built. The development of hotels and pleasure gardens overlooking Falmouth Bay and the beaches at Gyllyngvase (photo page 95) and Swanpool had to wait for the arrival of the railway in the 1860s. Traffic can be very congested in the busy summer months, so the easiest way into town is on the Park & Float/Park & Ride services from Ponsharden. A bus service runs to the Prince of Wales Pier (PWP), and the ferry from Ponsharden will drop you at Custom House Quay (CHQ) from where it is a short walk to the Maritime Museum and Discovery Quay (DQ). There are also large car parks on Pendennis Headland. If you are visiting by train, Falmouth Town halt is the closest to the Maritime Museum; Falmouth Docks station is closest to Pendennis Castle.

The Stack

Tuke's Beach

The Stack (Pennance Point) and Tuke's Beach

There was for many years a tall chimney standing prominently on the skyline above Pennance headland, and that is how it acquired its local name, The Stack. The chimney was connected by a long flue (still traceable in places) to an arsenic labyrinth on the cliffs below where lead and silver ore from Swanpool Mine was roasted. Arsenic was a valuable by-product sold as a pesticide to combat the cotton boll weevil in America (as children we were told never to eat the blackberries in this area because of the contamination). It's a pleasant walk out to Pennance Point where there are sweeping views over Falmouth Bay. Tuke's Beach is lovely shingle beach accessible from the coast path just past Stackpoint House. The painter Henry Scott Tuke (1858–1929) lived here and painted many nudes and maritime scenes in this area. His work is often on display at Falmouth Art Gallery.

Falmouth Docks

The main business is ship repair, and in the winter months the docks are packed with cross channel ferries. The eastern side of the docks is used for the building of luxury yachts and motor boats. There are fine views over to Trefusis from Castle Drive, the road that circumvents Pendennis Headland. A viewing area stands overlooking the main dry dock almost close enough to chat with someone on the ship's bridge. There is almost always an ice cream van parked here in the season.

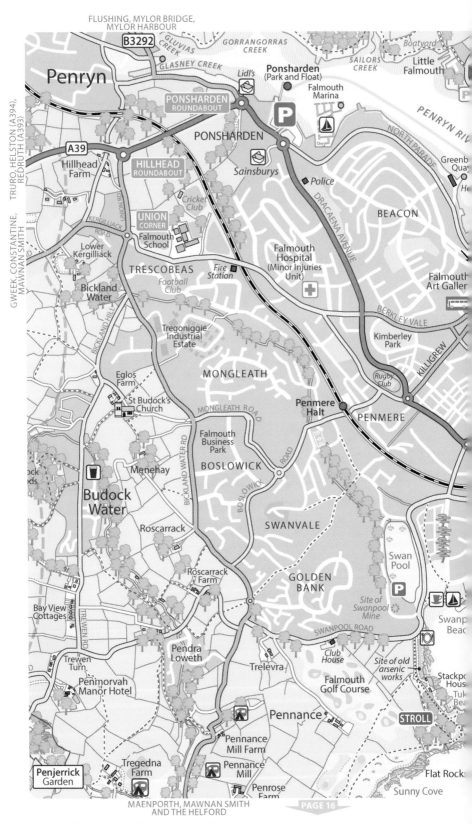

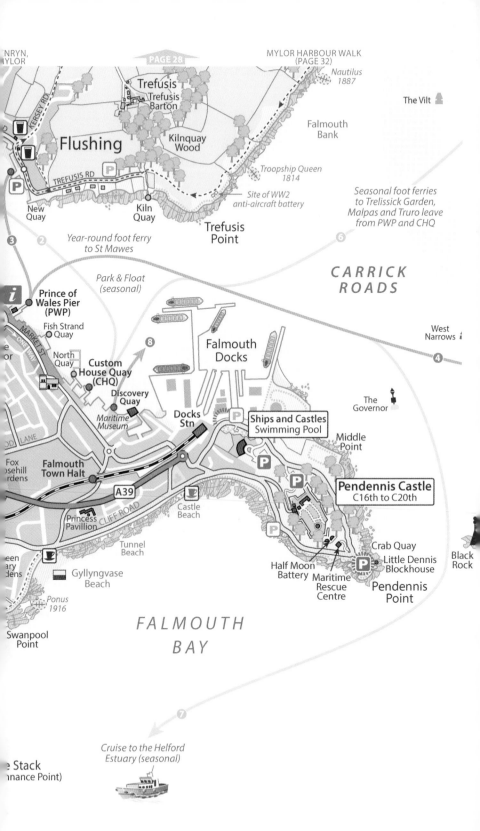

PAGE 28

MYLOR HARBOUR WALK
(PAGE 32)

*Nautilus
1887*

The Vilt

Trefusis

Trefusis
Barton

Kilnquay
Wood

Falmouth
Bank

Flushing

KERSEY RD

New
Quay

TREFUSIS RD

P

Kiln
Quay

*Troopship Queen
1814*

*Site of WW2
anti-aircraft battery*

**Trefusis
Point**

*Seasonal foot ferries
to Trelissick Garden,
Malpas and Truro leave
from PWP and CHQ*

3   2

*Year-round foot ferry
to St Mawes*

*Park & Float
(seasonal)*

*Prince of
Wales Pier
(PWP)*

Fish Strand
Quay

North
Quay

**Custom
House Quay
(CHQ)**

Discovery
Quay

*Maritime
Museum*

ONE WAY

MARKET ST

8

**Falmouth
Docks**

Docks
Stn

**CARRICK
ROADS**

West
Narrows *i*

4

The
Governor

Middle
Point

Ships and Castles
Swimming Pool

Pendennis Castle
C16th to C20th

Fox
osehill
rdens

**Falmouth
Town Halt**

A39

WOOD LANE

Princess
Pavillion

CLIFF ROAD

Castle
Beach

Tunnel
Beach

P

P

P

P

P

Crab Quay

Little Dennis
Blockhouse

Black
Rock

Half Moon
Battery

Maritime
Rescue
Centre

**Pendennis
Point**

een
ary
dens

Gyllyngvase
Beach

*Ponus
1916*

Swanpool
Point

**FALMOUTH
BAY**

7

*Cruise to the Helford
Estuary (seasonal)*

e Stack
nnance Point)

Pendennis Castle

Pendennis Castle

It is almost certain that there was a prehistoric fort here as the name Pendennis contains the Cornish word elements *pen* for *headland* and *dennis* for *castle*. Elizabethan and Civil War works seem to have destroyed any physical evidence of the prehistoric defences, and the castle we see today was commissioned in 1539 on the orders of Henry VIII in response to the threat of Spanish invasion. However, the limitations of early artillery meant that in order to defend Carrick Roads, cannons also had to be sited close to the water's edge at Little Dennis Blockhouse near Pendennis Point. The walls and moat were added to the main castle building by Elizabeth I in the 1590s following the invasion scare caused by the Spanish Armada in 1588. The indented shape of the defensive walls allows a clear shot on anyone attempting to scale them. The effectiveness of the design was proved in the English Civil War (1642–1651) by Sir John Arundell, the Royalist Governor of the castle who held out against a besieging Roundhead force for five months until forced to surrender because of starvation. It's said that when they marched out to surrender there was not a single rat or mouse left uneaten in the castle.

The walk around Pendennis Headland is a favourite for Falmouth residents. You simply follow the road that circles the headland to Little Dennis and Pendennis Point. You can also follow the moat most of the way around the castle, and children enjoy playing and exploring in the adjacent woods. There's a large car park for Pendennis Castle on the top of the headland (look out for the brown signs).

Pendennis Castle

Half Moon Battery

Half Moon Battery and the Maritime Rescue Coordination Centre
The Half Moon Battery was built at the beginning of the 20th
century on the site of an earlier Elizabethan (1558–1603) gun battery.
It has been restored and appears now as it would have done in
World War Two. The battery is accessed by tunnel from inside
Pendennis Castle (entrance fee). There is a twin emplacement on the
opposite side of the estuary at St Anthony (page 76). The modern
building just below is the Falmouth Maritime Rescue Coordination
Centre. It controls and coordinates search and rescue operations in the
Western Approaches.

Little Dennis Blockhouse and Pendennis Point
This circular gun tower (page 19) was hastily constructed following
a raid of Spanish ships that sailed unchallenged up river as far as
Truro in 1537. Like St Mawes Castle, its position on the water's edge
allows cannon shot to skim across the surface of the sea increasing
its range and striking any adversary in their most vulnerable point on
the waterline. Its location was also intended to deter an enemy ship
from trying to pass unchallenged beneath the guns in the main castle
above. Pendennis Point is a favourite spot to park, enjoy the views and
buy an ice cream. There is a picnic area here and at nearby Crab Quay.

Crab Quay Battery
A battery was first erected close to Crab Quay in 1795. It was rearmed
with quick-firing guns in 1940 to act as a defence against E-boats that
roamed in the English Channel. The gun positions and their magazines
are obvious, but below them, close to sea level, are the concrete bases
for searchlights used to illuminate any boat entering Carrick Roads at
night. On the rocks you can still make out the chains and eye bolts for
anti-submarine booms that closed the mouth of the estuary. The path
down to Crab Quay crosses over some old defensive trenches.

Carrick Roads

This broad expanse of sheltered water is one of the world's great anchorages, so big it's said a hundred sail ships could anchor in the many side creeks and corners without ever being in sight of each other. It takes its name from the Cornish word *karrek* for *rock* and presumably refers to either Carrick Carlys rock near Restronguet or, more probably, to Black Rock at the mouth of the estuary (page 92). Carrick Roads is rarely less than two kilometres wide and stretches six kilometres to Turnaware Bar where the narrower middle reaches of the estuary begin. The main deep channel snakes back and forth across Carrick Roads and is as much as 300 metres wide and 20 to 30 metres deep (presumably following the course of the old river when sea levels were lower in the last glacial period, 15,000 years ago). Either side of the deep channel it can be surprisingly shallow, sometimes with as little as a metre of water on the lowest tides. These shallow sandy banks are an ideal habitat for wild oysters, which have been harvested here for hundreds of years. The edge of the deep channel is marked by red and green buoys that guide the tugs towing ocean-going ships up to Tolverne and King Harry Reach for storage. The

Cormorant
(Shag similar but without the white face patch)

buoys are favourite places for cormorants and shags to perch and dry their outstretched wings between underwater fishing trips. Cormorants tend to favour the more sheltered parts of the estuary; their cousins the shags are more likely to found on the coast (dozens can often be seen on Shag Rock below St Anthony Lighthouse). Carrick Roads is best seen from the ferries that run to Trelissick, Malpas and Truro.

Black Rock

A local story tells how St Mawes, distracted by a seal whilst preaching, picked up a stone and hurled it at the seal, but he missed and the stone now forms Black Rock (photo page 92). Seals often haul themselves out and bask here at low water. The markings on the side of the beacon were used by gunners at Crab Quay Battery as datum points to calibrate their gun sights.

Grey Seal

Flushing, Trefusis Point, Enys and Mylor Harbour

Flushing

The busy hustle and bustle of Falmouth evaporates almost as soon as you step off the ferry at **Flushing Quay,** and within a few hundred metres you are into the open countryside or following the banks of Carrick Roads towards **Mylor Harbour.** This is the main base for oyster boats that work in Carrick Roads. Their tanbark sails are one of the great sights on the estuary in the autumn and winter. A little further inland (see map inside cover) at the head of the valley that falls to Mylor Creek is the beautiful **Enys House** and estate.

Flushing

The main street in Flushing is set back from the water, so there are only glimpses of the water between the elegant houses and where small slips meet the road. It's not full of shops and galleries like many coastal villages, but is a very pleasant place to wander. Until the 17th century this was just a small fishing hamlet called Nankersey set around a small creek. The Trefusis family wanted to develop it as a rival to Falmouth, and to that end they employed Dutch engineers to reclaim the foreshore, infilling Nankersey Creek (now Kersey Road) and building up the quays and sea walls so that the village took on the name of their home town, Flushing. However, it couldn't compete with Falmouth, and soon the quays were turned into gardens and it became a popular place for sea captains to live, allowing them and their families to steer clear of the rowdy streets of Falmouth. There is parking on the way into the village on St Peter's Road (if you see a space, just grab it) plus a tiny car park on Flushing Quay. It's easy to catch the regular year-round ferry from Prince of Wales Pier in Falmouth.

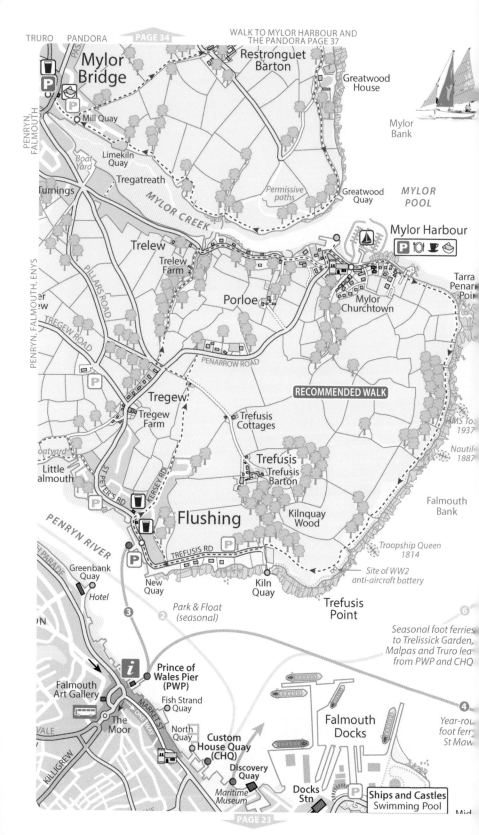

Mylor Bridge

Restronguet Barton

Greatwood House

Mylor Bank

PENRYN FALMOUTH

Mill Quay

Limekiln Quay

Boat Yard

Tregatreath

Turnings

MYLOR CREEK

Greatwood Quay

Permissive paths

MYLOR POOL

Trelew

Trelew Farm

Mylor Harbour

Tarra Penar Poi

PENRYN, FALMOUTH, ENYS

PILLARS ROAD

TREGEW ROAD

Porloe

Mylor Churchtown

PENARROW ROAD

RECOMMENDED WALK

HMS To
1937

Nautil
1887

Tregew

Tregew Farm

Trefusis Cottages

Trefusis

Trefusis Barton

Little almouth

Boatyard

ST PETER'S RD

KERSEY RD

Flushing

Kilnquay Wood

Falmouth Bank

PENRYN RIVER

TREFUSIS RD

Troopship Queen 1814

PARADE

Greenbank Quay

Hotel

New Quay

Kiln Quay

Site of WW2 anti-aircraft battery

Trefusis Point

3

2 Park & Float (seasonal)

6

Seasonal foot ferries to Trelissick Garden, Malpas and Truro lea from PWP and CHQ

Falmouth Art Gallery

i

Prince of Wales Pier (PWP)

Fish Strand Quay

MARKET ST

The Moor

North Quay

Custom House Quay (CHQ)

Discovery Quay

Maritime Museum

Falmouth Docks

Docks Stn

4

Year-rou foot ferr St Maw

Ships and Castles Swimming Pool

Mid

KILLIGREW

VALE

Mylor Churchtown and Mylor Harbour

The busy yacht harbour at Mylor sits next to a waterside church. The quay and buildings were constructed by the Royal Navy at the beginning of the 19th century to provision and repair ships anchored in Mylor and St Just Pool. Old naval hulks were moored here and used as training ships for young recruits and, as a result, a surprising number of old ships of the line survived in Carrick Roads into the 20th century. They include the famous *HMS Trincomolee*, launched in 1817 and now berthed at the National Museum of the Royal Navy in Hartlepool, and *HMS Implacable*, which fought at Trafalgar in 1805. The French Resistance used Mylor as a base for clandestine raids into occupied France during World War Two.

The church is dedicated to St Mylor, the son of Melainus, a Dark Age (AD410–1000) King of Cornwall. He was only seven when his uncle murdered his father and seized the throne. His uncle intended to kill the boy but was dissuaded and instead cut off Mylor's right hand and his left foot, exiling him to the abbey at Quimper in Brittany (at this time there were very close cultural links between Cornwall and Brittany). In Quimper his missing right hand was replaced by one made of silver and his leg by one of bronze. Miraculously these metal limbs worked as if they were natural, and by the time Mylor was fourteen, his fame had spread beyond Brittany. His uncle, fearing he would return to claim the throne of Cornwall, sent an assassin to kill him and the boy was decapitated. The assassin died three days after touching Mylor's severed head. Mylor's cult grew and spread back to Cornwall.

The five-metre-high cross that stands south of the church was discovered buried upside down acting as a buttress to one of the walls. If you count the two metres buried below ground, this is one of the tallest crosses in Cornwall – its only rival being the cross at St Clement Church. Local tradition claims it as the marker of St Mylor's grave but it may be much older, possibly a Bronze Age (2300–800BC) menhir or standing stone. It could have been standing here for 2,500 years before the church you see today was even built. Early Christians made a point of reappropriating pagan sacred sites and the objects they found at them. This possible menhir has been reworked with a pattern of circles and whorls typical of medieval Celtic crosses.

HMS Implacable in Carrick Roads

Oyster boat

The Oyster Fishery

The shallow shingle bed of Carrick Roads is an ideal habitat for native wild oysters. At the moment there are about ten sailboats that work the oyster beds, and Mylor Harbour is home to most of them. Mechanical aids are prohibited so dredging is done by hand using only the power of wind and tide, a technique that hasn't changed for hundreds of years. In the shallower places, dredging is carried out by small rowing punts that pull themselves between two opposing anchors hauling a small dredge along the seabed as they go (page 37). The season lasts from the beginning of October to the end of March. Oysters caught during the winter are fattened up over the summer in lays in the smaller creeks ready for the Falmouth Oyster Festival in October.

Trefusis Point and the wreck of the troopship *Queen*

In mid-January 1814, after enduring a rough passage from Lisbon, the troopship *Queen* called in at Falmouth for some respite. She was returning from the Peninsular War (1807–1814) in Spain with more than 300 wounded soldiers and crew on board. Carrick Roads is a famously sheltered anchorage and the *Queen* only let out a single anchor. However, it is vulnerable to gales from the south, which are able to blow unhindered up the estuary. So on the evening of the 13th January, when gale-force winds suddenly turned southerly, the *Queen* was caught unprepared. The lone anchor started to drag and her high sides were caught by the wind, forcing her towards the shore in a flurry of snow showers and squalls. The ship, already in a poor condition, disintegrated almost as soon as she touched the bottom, throwing many panic-stricken passengers and crew straight into the sea. The collapsed rigging provided an escape route to the shore for some, but many more were washed towards Pencarrow Point (Cornish for *headland of the dead*). As dawn rose on the 14th January, the scale of loss became apparent – whole rafts of bodies could be made out and many of the drowned were still tangled in the rigging. More than 250 died and, gruesomely, some of the survivors were caught robbing the corpses. There is a carved memorial in Mylor Churchyard.

Bluebells at Enys

Enys House and Garden

The house that stands today is the third on this site. It replaced an Elizabethan manor lost to fire in 1826. The new house was designed in the pared back Georgian style of the 1830s, and it's the most beautiful house on the Fal Estuary. Enys was requisitioned in World War Two as a training establishment for the Royal Netherlands Navy and then served for a short while as a school. From the end of the 1950s it was uninhabited and gradually fell into disrepair, its interior suffering damage from water ingress. Restoration started in the 1980s and

Enys House

necessitated the removal of areas of the plaster walls and ceilings, intriguingly exposing parts of the structure beneath. The rooms have little furniture or decoration and that allows the elegance of the underlying proportions to shine through. Woodland walks take you down to a pond, and the grounds are particularly loved for the display of bluebells and ramsons at the beginning of May, known as Bluebell Week, when people travel from all over Cornwall to visit. It's not open every day, so check opening times before you travel.

Mylor boats dredging for oysters in Carrick Roads

Parking, shorter walks and leisurely strolls

Mylor Harbour has a large car park plus a little roadside parking by the church. There's a free car park opposite Mylor Stores in the centre of **Mylor Bridge** plus a little parking at Trevellan Road/Mill Quay. **Flushing** has roadside parking on St Peter's Road as far as the Royal Standard plus a few places near the quay. There is roadside parking on Trefusis Road near **Kiln Quay** – drive through Flushing. As usual in the busy summer months, if you see a space, grab it.

Both **Flushing** and **Mylor Harbour** are good places for a short stroll and from both you can walk a little way on the coast. The garden at **Enys** is always a good place to stroll.

A walk from Flushing to Mylor Harbour

*A circular walk which can be started in **Flushing**, **Mylor Bridge** or **Mylor Harbour**. A regular year-round foot ferry runs from Falmouth to Flushing Quay and that's where we start.*

From **Flushing Quay** head north (left) along **Trefusis Road** past Flushing Stores and the Seven Stars pub to where **Kersey Road** leaves on the right by the Royal Standard pub. Walk along Kersey Road for about 300m and look for a small path and steps that leave on the left just before **Orchard Vale** and **Kersey Close**. The path follows the hedge, crossing a field to join the driveway to Trefusis Barton. Turn left and after 100m you will come to the public road.

Keep straight ahead (as if to Mylor Bridge) and after 50m a path leaves the road on the right that crosses fields and eventually takes you down to the creekside road at **Trelew**. Turn right for **Mylor Harbour** where you will find a cafe, bistro and loos.

To return to Flushing, follow the road past Castaways Bistro. A path then follows the shore all the way to **Kiln Quay** where there's a small beach. Follow **Trefusis Road** back into **Flushing**.

....

Distance
6.1km (3¾ miles).

Food and drink
Flushing and Mylor Harbour have a choice of places to eat. You could also try the Lemon Arms in Mylor Bridge.

Flushing

Restronguet, Pandora Inn, Mylor Bridge and Kennall Vale

Greatwood Quay

This section is a tale of two creeks – **Restronguet Creek** that follows the Carnon Valley and was once the major route into and out of the great copper and tin mining district around Gwennap, and the much smaller **Mylor Creek**. The promontory of land that separates them has two delightful places to visit, the **Pandora Inn** at **Restronguet Passage** and the quay below **Greatwood**. We have also added **Kennall Vale Gunpowder Mills** near Ponsanooth, a wildlife reserve now but once part of the great industrial infrastructure of this area.

Mylor Creek, Mylor Bridge and Greatwood Quay

The medieval main road from Penryn to Truro crossed Mylor Bridge on its way to the old ferry crossing at Restronguet Passage (this was before Falmouth was established). A small settlement developed around a boatyard and corn mills including, until the end of the 18th century, a tidal mill like those on the Roseland (page 79). The valley continues inland to Enys House (page 31). From Mylor Bridge a path follows the water's edge to Greatwood Quay built in the 18th century for the export of copper ore brought here by mule trains. It's a good place to stop for a picnic on a walk to Restronguet Passage.

Restronguet Creek and the Pandora Inn

Restronguet comes from the Cornish word elements *ros* for *spur* or *headland* and *tron-gos* for *nose-wood* and presumably refers to Restronguet Point, which comes close to blocking the mouth of the creek. The creek is fed by streams that originate on the granite high ground to the west and pass through the rich tin and copper mining district of Gwennap Parish, once described as the 'richest

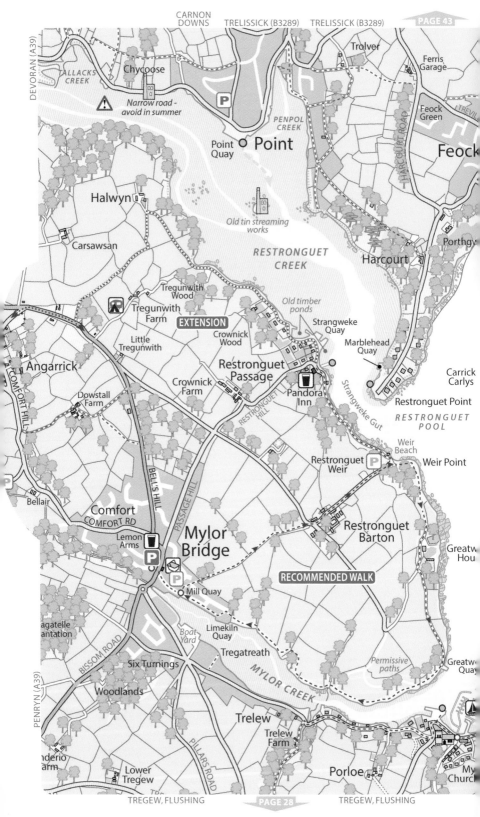

DEVORAN (A39)

TALLACKS CREEK

Chycoose

⚠ Narrow road - avoid in summer

P

PENPOL CREEK

Trolver

Ferris Garage

Feock Green

Point Quay ○ Point

Feock

Halwyn

Old tin streaming works

RESTRONGUET CREEK

Porthgv

Harcourt

Carsawsan

Tregunwith Wood

Old timber ponds

Strangweke Quay

Marblehead Quay

Carrick Carlys

Tregunwith Farm

EXTENSION

Crownick Wood

Little Tregunwith

Angarrick

Crownick Farm

Restronguet Passage

Strangweke Gut

Restronguet Point

RESTRONGUET POOL

COMFORT HILL

Dowstall Farm

Pandora Inn

RESTRONGUET HILL

Weir Beach

Weir Point

P

Restronguet Weir

P

Bellair

BELL'S HILL

Comfort

COMFORT RD

Restronguet Barton

Greatw Hou

Lemon Arms

P

PASSAGE HILL

Mylor Bridge

P

RECOMMENDED WALK

P

○ Mill Quay

Boat Yard

Limekiln Quay

Permissive paths

Greatw Quay

BISSOM ROAD

agatelle antation

PENRYN (A39)

Six Turnings

Tregatreath

MYLOR CREEK

Woodlands

Trelew

PILLARS ROAD

Trelew Farm

derio arm

Lower Tregew

Porloe

My Church

square mile on Earth'. In the past, streams that cut across the tin veins eroded and transported the particles of ore, depositing it in dark layers in the river bed further down stream. These easily exploited deposits of stream tin attracted the metal smiths of the Bronze Age (2300–800BC), and they were the first to sift and pan the river sediments using deer antlers as picks (there's one in the Royal Cornwall Museum in Truro). That activity continued on and off into the Elizabethan period (1558–1603), the deposits being continuously reworked to recover lower and lower concentrations of tin. Activity peaked in the mid 19th century when an artificial island was created in the middle of Restronguet Creek. A shaft was sunk into the gravel to mine the previously out of reach deposits, which are as much as five metres below the river bed here. At low water you can just make out the small island in the middle of the creek where the shaft was located.

As the stream tin became worked out so attention turned to exploiting the mineral veins themselves, but efforts were severely hampered by the hardness of the rock and it was only with the refinement of gunpowder in the 18th and 19th centuries (see Kennall Vale overleaf) that the lodes could be blasted out and followed underground. At that point mining boomed, and this small creek became lined with quays for export of ore and the import of timber props and coal for the pumping engines. Hundreds of years of turning over the riverbed to extract stream tin plus mine waste that has flowed into the creek, have silted up the Carnon Valley so that the tide now only flows as far as Devoran. The Mineral Tramways that brought ore to the quays at Devoran and Point now form part of a network of cycle paths that run to Redruth and Portreath on the north coast.

The Pandora Inn is one of the loveliest settings for any pub on the estuary, and sitting out on the pontoon at night is one of the great things to do in the area. The pub exists here because at one time the medieval main road from Penryn to King Harry and Truro crossed Restronguet Creek by ferry at this point. The inn is said to be named after *HMS Pandora*, the ship that searched the Pacific for the mutineers of the *Bounty*. The captain of the *Pandora* is reputedly a former landlord. Nearby Strangweke Quay was built to serve ships that were too large to reach the quays further up at Point and Devoran. Timber pit props from Scandinavia were stored in large ponds on either side of the quay – the line of which can still be made out in the creek. The salt water acted as a preservative on the wood, which was stored here for up to a year. Parking at Restronguet Passage is almost all reserved for customers of the Pandora Inn, and is often full in the summer.

Kennall Vale

Kennall Vale Gunpowder Mills

The fast-flowing Kennall River starts life on the high ground above Stithians and feeds into Restronguet Creek opposite Devoran. The gunpowder mills in Kennall Vale were built by the Fox family at the beginning of the 19th century to produce gunpowder for the booming copper and tin mining industry. At their height in the 1850s the mills employed 70 men, women and boys. The entrance track follows the south side of the valley to a more recent granite quarry and ends abruptly in a massive blast wall that runs across the whole width of the valley. This was designed to protect the paper mills in the valley above from the periodic accidents and explosions in the gunpowder mills. The mills stand in pairs on the north side of the valley and were powered by large water wheels fed by leats drawn off the river higher up the valley. It was here the gunpowder ingredients were ground together between limestone mill stones. The mills were designed with thick, massive walls and very lightweight roofs, so that if an explosion happened, the force would be directed upwards, limiting the damage (and danger) to the rest of the site. Accidents were not uncommon, and in 1838 five mills blew up one after the other, propelling slates to the edge of Ponsanooth village. Towards the end of the 19th century the demand for gunpowder declined and more powerful (and safer) explosives like dynamite were preferred (manufactured at Hayle Towans in West Cornwall), and this site closed at the end of World War One. To get here take the A393 towards Redruth from Treluswell Roundabout. As you come down the hill in Ponsanooth you pass the Stag Hunt pub, and the road turns sharply to the right and crosses a bridge. Just after the bridge turn left into Park Road by the village shop. Follow the road for 200m past the school, and as the road turns up Cot Hill, look for somewhere to park on the left in Kennall Vale Road (there's no parking at the reserve). The entrance to the nature reserve is about 150m up Cot Hill, opposite Cotwood Cottage. Kennall Vale is owned by Cornwall Wildlife Trust; they have a downloadable leaflet that covers the history of the site and the wildlife that lives here.

Restronguet Point looking over to the Pandora Inn

Parking, shorter walks and leisurely strolls

There is some very limited parking at **Restronguet Passage** but it is mostly for customers of the **Pandora Inn** and, even for them, it's often difficult to find space here in the summer. One option, if there is a large group of you, is to arrive by water taxi. There is a car park in the centre of **Mylor Bridge** opposite Mylor Stores and a little more space on **Mill Quay** (take Trevellan Road just before Mylor Stores). There is roadside parking for 10 cars just above **Weir Beach**.

There are popular creekside strolls in either direction from the **Pandora Inn** and **Weir Beach**. You can shortcut over the fields south of Greatwood Quay back to the public road.

A walk from Mylor Bridge to the Pandora Inn and back by Greatwood Quay

*This walk starts in **Mylor Bridge** (parking at Restronguet Passage is very limited), then crosses inland to **Restronguet Barton** and **Weir Beach**. There you have a choice to head to the **Pandora Inn** (and possibly a longer walk to Halwyn) or to return to Mylor Bridge by **Greatwood Quay**, a good place to stop and picnic.*

Park in the car park just before the Lemon Arms in **Mylor Bridge**. Walk back to the road. Just down from the shop you'll see **Trevellan Road**; walk 200m to **Mill Quay**. Just at the end of Mill Quay the road starts to rise (at this point the waterside path you will return on is signposted straight ahead). Leave the road here by turning left and inland and up a small tarmac lane that soon becomes a green tree-lined track and then a path in a field. Keep the hedge on your right until you meet the public road at **Restronguet Barton**. Follow the road straight ahead and down the hill to **Weir Beach**.

Turn left at **Weir Beach** for the Pandora Inn, otherwise turn right to return to **Mylor Bridge**. Follow the track as it rises behind **Greatwood House** and continues to **Greatwood Quay** (photo page 33). The path then follows Mylor Creek back to the start point.

A longer walk from the Pandora Inn follows Restronguet Creek to Halwyn and then up to the public road (blue dotted line on map). At the road turn left to follow the main road back to Mylor Bridge (Bell's Hill), or right and then first left to return by a quiet, leafy road past Angarrick and down Comfort Hill.

Distance
3.3km (2 miles) round trip, add 1.5km to go to the Pandora Inn for lunch.
Extension to Halwyn returning down Bell's Hill or by Comfort adds 3.5km (2¼ miles).

Food and drink
Lemon Arms and shop in Mylor Bridge, Pandora Inn at Restronguet Passage.

Oyster punt

Looking over the Tresillian River on the path between Malpas and St Clement (Denas Road)

2. Truro, Trelissick and the Upper Reaches
Creeks abandoned by the falling tide

BEYOND TURNAWARE BAR, THE WIDE VIEWS and open skies so characteristic of Carrick Roads are left behind and, for the first time, we encounter the thickly wooded creeks of the middle and upper reaches of the estuary – principally the Fal, Truro and Tresillian rivers. The transition is surprisingly abrupt as the estuary, still two kilometres wide near Restronguet Point, is suddenly compressed between tall banks little more than 200 metres apart. In these middle reaches between Trelissick and Malpas, the currents constrained between the banks scour the main channel so that at King Harry Reach ocean-going ships are able to moor two abreast just a stone's throw from the bank. Their huge rudders and propellers loom over passing ferries lending a surreal note to this part of the estuary.

The National Trust house and garden at **Trelissick** with its popular woodland walks are the major attraction in this area. It's also a good starting point for longer walks to Roundwood Quay and the hamlets at Cowlands and Coombe. These are heavenly places with plum and apple orchards draped over the water's edge. When the early morning mist hangs over the river (page 6) their dreamy atmosphere is heightened by the muffled sounds that drift in from the busy main channel, particularly the clank, clank, clank of the King Harry Ferry as it draws itself along on the great iron chains fixed between the river banks.

Just opposite Tolverne Passage the main channel splits; the River Fal bears east along Ruan Creek to Ruan Lanihorne and the **Truro River** heads north past Old Kea to Malpas. The Truro River is busy with passing ferries and yachts in the summer but its banks remain largely private and inaccessible. The only exceptions are the old ferry landing beaches at Halwyn and Kea Wood, which are both served by footpaths. The eastern bank is dominated by

HIGHLIGHTS
TRELISSICK
Woodland walks, walled garden, gallery and cafe.
COWLANDS CREEK
The prettiest creek on the west side of the estuary.

USEFUL FERRIES
Check the Fal River website for timetables, latest information and updates. Main ferry landing places are marked ● on the maps. Other potential landing places are marked ○.

Seasonal foot ferries Ⓕ from Falmouth and St Mawes call at Trelissick Garden on their way to Town Quay, Truro. If the tide is too low to reach Truro the ferry lands at Malpas instead where there is a connecting bus. From Malpas you can walk to St Clement (page 54) and/or visit the Heron Inn, but check that the ferry picks up at Malpas for your return trip.

BOAT HIRE
Motor boat, kayak and sailboat hire from Loe Beach. You might find someone at Malpas boatyard willing to drop you at Kea Wood from where you can walk to Cowlands and Trelissick.

Cowlands (Coombe) Creek

the **Tregothnan Estate**, an area broadly defined by the courses of the Fal, Truro and Tresillian rivers. This secluded area has few paths and little access to the waterside, but for the dedicated explorer of the estuary there are some really characterful hidden corners to visit: the ruined church of St Coan at Merther, the old ferry landing at Malpas Point (page 54) or the quays at Ruan Lanihorne. In the autumn, the woods around Lamorran are one of the great sights of the river as the oak leaves turn beautiful hues of yellow and orange. The easily navigable middle reaches of the estuary end at Malpas where the estuary splits again. The Truro River turns west towards Calenick and Sunny Corner; the Tresillian River heads east past the hamlet at St Clement and on to the tidal limit at Tresillian.

The final area covered in this chapter takes us back to Tolverne Passage to follow the River Fal as it heads east along **Ruan Creek** to Sett Bridge and Ruan Lanihorne. Almost as soon as it splits from the Truro River it starts to lose depth and, despite its width, the creek rapidly fills with mud and sand banks. It was not always like this and the tide once reached much further inland than today's tidal limit at Ruan Lanihorne. In the Iron Age (800BC–AD43) and Roman period, flat-bottomed Roman and Phoenician trading ships could make it past Tregony to the Iron Age fort at Golden near Trewithen to trade fine tableware for ingots of tin smelted from the local river gravels. A thousand years of digging over the river bed for stream tin filled the creek with silt so that by 1300, the tidal limit had migrated downstream to Tregony. More recently, waste from the great china clay pits of St Stephen and St Dennis has added more material and the tide now only reaches as far as Sett Bridge. Ruan Creek is the quietest part of the whole estuary and access is limited to areas around Ruan Lanihorne and to a single path from Philleigh (page 61). On these upper reaches (and beyond Malpas on the Truro and Tresillian rivers), you really do start to feel a long way from the sea. When the tide is out these broad creeks take on a melancholy air as the falling tide reveals great expanses of mud and the skeletal ribs of long abandoned boats.

Trelissick, Roundwood Quay, Feock and Loe Beach

King Harry Reach

At **Loe Beach**, **Feock** and **Trelissick** there is one last chance to take in the views of Carrick Roads and the open sea before we enter the more enclosed middle and upper reaches of the estuary. The National Trust house at **Trelissick** is one of the most visited places on the estuary. Children love running in the woods and marvel at the sight of the ocean-going ships moored close to the shore at **King Harry Reach**. After a stomp through the woods everyone can be revived at the cafe. Just a little further north of Trelissick's woodland walks, **Roundwood Quay** sits inside an Iron Age fort on Lamouth Creek.

Feock and Loe Beach

While Feock is not on the main visitor trail, it is one of the loveliest and most sought-after places to live near the river. The road through the village is narrow with only few places to stop, but you can park in the Church Hall car park and follow the track down to Pill Creek (there's also a path a little further on just past Creek House). Loe Beach is used by local families in the summer, but it's mainly a base for water sports and you can hire out kayaks, paddleboards and motor and sail boats for exploring the river. It's a popular place to bird watch for winter visitors from Iceland, the Baltic and Scandinavia, particularly grebes and divers. A small pay car park and cafe sit at the top of the beach.

King Harry Ferry

This busy ferry crossing to and from the Roseland saves nearly thirty kilometres on the alternative land route via Tresillian and Tregony. There's just enough time as the ferry crosses the river to get out of your car and take in the view. You will need cash for the fare.

Trelissick

Trelissick House and Garden
The woodland walks are very popular with families. They can be extended north to Roundwood Quay and even to the pretty hamlets of Cowlands and Coombe. Trelissick House has a lovely walled garden, cafe and gallery showing the work of local artists and craftsmen. The woodland walks, walled garden, tea rooms and gallery are open year round; the house is open on selected days. Trelissick has its own pontoon served by ferries from Truro, St Mawes and Falmouth.

Lamouth Creek, Roundwood Quay and fort
The promontory fort at Roundwood was built in the latter part of the Iron Age (800BC–AD43) and was probably in use into the Romano-British period (AD43–410) presumably as a place to trade tin and other goods. The landward side is defended by a pair of earth ramparts presumably once topped by a timber palisade. The original entrance is in the centre of the ramparts a little south of the modern track. A large oval, possibly older, earthwork sits inside the ramparts. The site has the advantage of being close to, but almost hidden from, the main river. The quays were built in the late 18th century to serve the expanding copper mines of Chacewater and Gwennap. Copper ore was brought overland by pack horse to be shipped to Wales for smelting; coal and timber for the mines were imported in return. The opening of the Redruth and Chacewater Railway in 1826, with its termination at Devoran on Restronguet Creek, ended this trade and the quays were subsequently used for ship building and exporting agricultural produce. Today they are a great place to stop for a picnic, and the National Trust have opened up further footpaths from the track to the public road. You can park at Trelissick and walk down through Namphillows Wood, or at the lay-by at Feock Turn. There is a tiny lay-by near Tregew Farm where there is room for a couple of cars.

Kingfisher

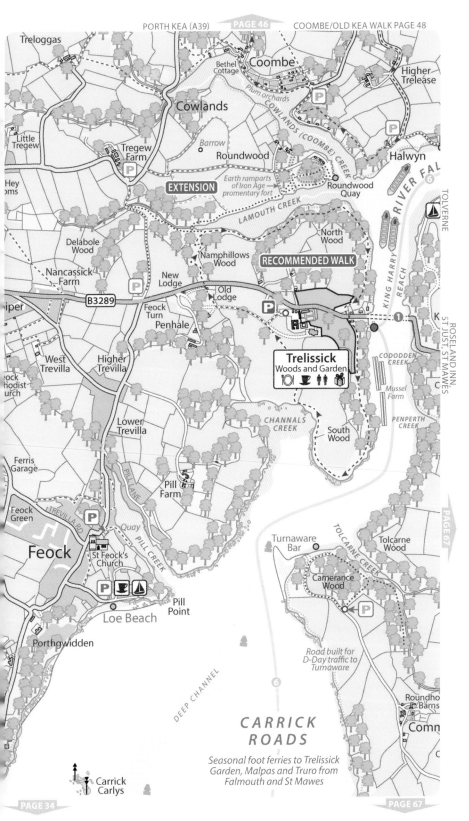

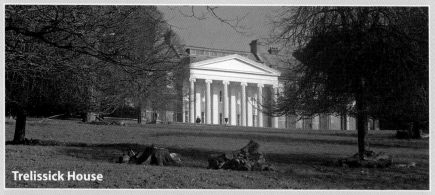

Trelissick House

Parking, shorter walks and leisurely strolls

You can arrive at **Trelissick** by seasonal ferry ⑥ from **Falmouth**, **St Mawes** or **Truro**. After landing you have the option of visiting the house, gallery and garden or walking through the woods. There's plenty of parking at **Trelissick** itself.

As for roadside parking, there are about 10 spaces in the lay-by opposite **Feock Turn** near Trelissick. This is a good starting point for the walk to **Roundwood Quay** (shown on the map as a dotted blue line) or a longer walk to **Cowlands** and **Coombe**. There are also one or two roadside parking spaces near **Tregew Farm** (but you're likely to find them taken in the busy summer months).

A circular walk through Trelissick Woods to Lamouth Creek and King Harry Passage

*This circular woodland walk is probably the most popular in this book (although it's rarely crowded). The whole walk is quite long so smaller children might prefer a shorter walk through **Namphillows Wood** to **Roundwood Quay** and back.*

Park at **Trelissick House**. From the car park head south (away from the road entrance) looking for signs to the woodland walk. They will direct you through a hedge, over a cattle grid and onto a driveway. Turn right on the driveway as it curves through the parkland away from the house. After about 300m the parkland gives way to woods and, as you cross another cattle grid, a path leaves on the right signed for the woodland walk. You will come to the **Old Lodge**. Cross the main road and follow the path down through **Namphillows Wood** to **Lamouth Creek**. At the creekside turn right for the longer circular woodland walk (or left and over the footbridge for the shorter walk to Roundwood). From here on it's clear going, the only slight difficulty being the steep climb in and out of the valley at **King Harry Passage** where you have to cross the traffic queuing for the ferry.

Distance
4.3km (2¾ miles) round trip.

Food and drink
Teas and loos at Trelissick, Punchbowl and Ladle pub and Linden Hey Garden Tea Rooms at nearby Penelewey on the B3289.

The pontoon at Trelissick and the King Harry Ferry

Old Kea, Coombe, Halwyn and Cowlands Creek

Ferry on its way to Malpas

This is the one of prettiest corners of the estuary, neatly tucked into the elbow of the Truro River as it heads first to Malpas and then turns west to Calenick and Truro. This part of the estuary is less visited than Trelissick and Roundwood because parking is scarce (although you can easily walk here from Trelissick). **Cowlands Creek** is one of the loveliest creeks on the estuary matched only by the Percuil River on the Roseland. A creekside path links the hamlets at **Cowlands** and **Coombe**, and there is also the opportunity to visit two old ferry landings that once served vicars and agricultural workers – one below **Halwyn** and one below **Kea Wood** (page 54).

Old Kea Church and St Kea

Kea Church's isolated location on the extreme east of its large straggling parish meant it was abandoned in 1802 for a new, more conveniently sited church at Kea five kilometres east, and the church here is now roofless (like nearby Merther on the Tresillian River). The site is of great age and may once have been a Celtic monastery. St Kea is said to have floated here from Ireland in a stone trough in the 5th or 6th century, founding this church where he landed. He was famed for his love of animals and is said to have shielded a stag being hunted by King Teudar and his nobles. The grateful stag allowed Kea to harness him to pull a plough. A single parson served both this parish and St Michael Penkevil on the other side of the river, commuting by rowing punt between Parson's and Church Creek. There's a little roadside parking by Churchtown Farm and from here you can walk to Halwyn and Coombe or stroll down to the river through Kea Wood.

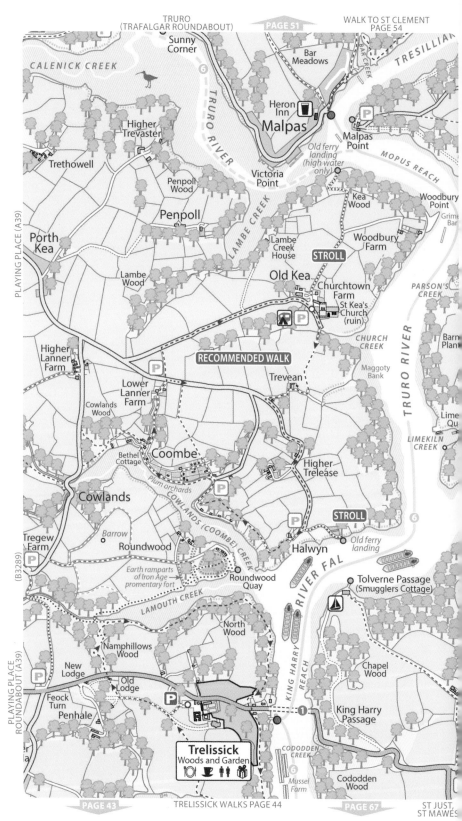

CALENICK CREEK

Sunny
Corner

Bar
Meadows

TRESILLIAN

Higher
Trevaster

Heron
Inn

Malpas

Malpas
Point

Trethowell

Old ferry
landing (high water
only)

MOPUS REACH

Penpoll
Wood

Victoria
Point

Kea
Wood

Woodbury
Point

Grime
Bar

PLAYING PLACE (A39)

Penpoll

Porth
Kea

LAMBE CREEK

Lambe
Creek
House

Woodbury
Farm

Lambe
Wood

STROLL

Old Kea

TRURO RIVER

PARSON'S
CREEK

Churchtown
Farm

St Kea's
Church
(ruin)

CHURCH
CREEK

Barn
Plan

Higher
Lanner
Farm

RECOMMENDED WALK

Trevean

Maggoty
Bank

Lime
Qu

LIMEKILN
CREEK

Lower
Lanner
Farm

Cowlands
Wood

Bethel
Cottage

Coombe

Higher
Trelease

Plum orchards

Cowlands

COWLANDS (COOMBE) CREEK

STROLL

Tregew
Farm

(B3289)

Barrow

Roundwood

Halwyn

Old ferry
landing

Tolverne Passage
(Smugglers Cottage)

Earth ramparts
of Iron Age
promentary fort

Roundwood
Quay

RIVER FAL

LAMOUTH CREEK

North
Wood

KING HARRY REACH

Chapel
Wood

Namphillows
Wood

New
Lodge

Old
Lodge

King Harry
Passage

PLAYING PLACE
ROUNDABOUT (A39)

Feock
Turn

Penhale

Trelissick
Woods and Garden

CODODDEN
CREEK

Mussel
Farm

Cododden
Wood

46 | *Old Kea, Coombe, Halwyn and Cowlands Creek*

Kea plum

Kea Wood

A ferry once operated from below Kea Wood, and although it's rarely, if ever, used now you can follow a public path from Old Kea down to the landing beach (page 54). There is a heronry in Kea Wood and the birds are a common sight peering out of the trees on the middle reaches of the estuary. They are sensitive to disturbance so try to stay on the path and keep dogs on a lead. If you do arrange to be picked up here, make sure it's on a high tide as the muddy banks are impassable at low water.

Cowlands Creek, Coombe and Kea plums

This is the most beautiful creek on the western side of the estuary with pretty waterside cottages and banks planted with orchards of Kea plums. The small fruits, a cross between a wild sloe and cultivated varieties of damson, are mainly used for jam-making. The trees like these sheltered south-facing banks and seem unconcerned to have their roots in the salty water. Kea plums are having a revival and new orchards are being planted. You can buy jars of jam and chutney online from the Tregothnan website (Tregothnan Estate own much of the land here) and in the summer and autumn from outside cottages in Coombe. A footpath follows the creek between Cowlands and Coombe and then through the woods to Halwyn. There's space for a few cars to park on the roadside at Coombe.

Halwyn and the old ferry to Tolverne

A ferry used to run from Halwyn to the thatched ferry cottage at Tolverne Passage. There is parking for two cars near Halwyn opposite the track that takes you down to the small landing beach. Tolverne Passage, like Turnaware Bar (page 66), was an embarkation point for troops heading for the D-Day landings in 1944. For many years it was called the Smuggler's Cottage and was a popular ferry stop for tea and scones. It's now a boatyard.

The ferry at Tolverne

Looking over to Tolverne from near Halwyn as the early morning mist lifts

Parking, shorter walks and leisurely strolls

Parking is in short supply in this area. There's space for a couple of cars on the road and at the top of the beach at **Coombe** (beware the returning tide). One or two roadside spaces at **Lower Lanner**, **Old Kea Church** and at **Halwyn** (opposite the track that leads to the old ferry landing) and a couple of spaces near **Tregew Farm**. It's quite possible for all of these to be taken so be prepared to look for alternatives.

In the busy summer months there's a better chance of parking at the lay-by at **Feock Turn** near Trelissick or at **Trelissick** itself. You can arrive at **Trelissick** by seasonal ferry ⑥ from **Falmouth**, **St Mawes** or **Truro**.

A walk from Old Kea to Halwyn, Coombe and Cowlands Creek

*The hamlet of **Coombe** with its creekside plum orchards is the great attraction of this walk. There are views over the main river as well as lovely **Cowlands Creek**. It involves walking on narrow, but little used public roads. There is an option to walk down through **Kea Wood** or the old ferry landing below **Halwyn**. Parking is scarce so take it where you find it rather than pinning your hopes on any one location.*

Park on the road near **Old Kea Church**. Walk past the old church to the head of **Church Creek**. Cross the stream and follow the path over the field and up the hill (ignoring the farm track on your right). Aim to the left of the buildings at **Trevean Barn**. You will come

to a farm track, turn right past **Trevean** and after 300m you'll join the public road. Turn left here and follow the road to **Halwyn**. The track down to the river and old landing place leaves the road on the corner just opposite the tiny lay-by for 2 cars and 25m before the end of the public road. To continue to **Coombe** follow the footpath signs at **Halwyn** and you are back into fields and woods to **Coombe**.

At low water in **Coombe** you can follow the path at the top of the foreshore but there is an inland diversion through the orchards if needed. After about 500m from Coombe and just after **Bethel Cottage** a small stream joins the creek near the house called **Turn-a-penny**. Turn inland here to **Lower Lanner** and back to the public road. Once on the road look for the path opposite the entrance to Lower Lanner Farm; cross a single field (or follow the road around) to join the road to **Old Kea** and back to the start.

Distance
4.9km (3 miles) round trip.

Food and drink
Teas and toilets at Trelissick, Punchbowl and Ladle pub and Linden Hey Garden Tea Rooms at Penelewey.

Cowlands Creek

Truro, Malpas and St Clement

St Clement

The Truro and Tresillian rivers merge at **Malpas,** which sits at the head of the middle reaches of the estuary – where the main channel remains navigable even at low water. In the past, larger ships would dock or anchor in Mopus Reach and transfer their cargo to flat-bottomed barges to proceed to the quays in **Truro** and **Tresillian**. Today, seasonal ferries land at Malpas on a low tide, when it's too shallow to make it all the way to Town Quay in Truro. You can then walk to **St Clement** or simply sit out at the Heron Inn and enjoy the views.

Truro

In common with the older towns on the estuary like Penryn and Tregony, Truro owes its existence to its position at the furthest part of the tidal estuary from the open sea, being able to draw in business from central Cornwall. Warehouses once lined the whole river front from Newham into the city centre at Lemon Quay (now a public square). There are still some lovely little corners tucked beside the cathedral that hint at how the old town appeared. It prospered in the 17th and 18th centuries on the boom in copper and tin mining, and this was when the elegant Georgian houses in Lemon Street and Boscawen Square were built. Today, Truro is Cornwall's administrative and shopping centre, and many shoppers travel to Truro for the range of smaller independent shops. For those not wanting to shop there is the Royal Cornwall Museum and Truro Cathedral to visit. Ferries from Falmouth and St Mawes bring you right into the centre of the city at Town Quay but can only reach here on a high tide. When the water is too low, a bus takes you to and from Malpas to pick up the ferry.

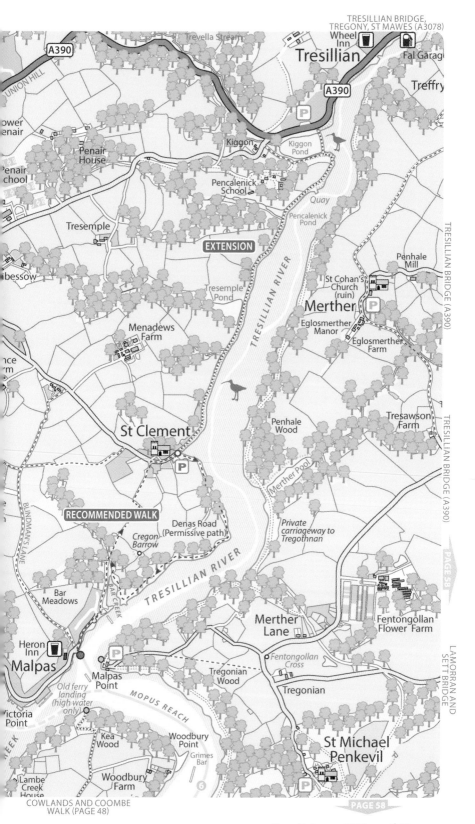

A390

Trevella Stream

Wheel
Inn

Tresillian

Fal Garage

A390

Treffry

UNION HILL

ower
enair

Penair
House

Kiggon

Kiggon
Pond

enair
chool

Pencalenick
School

Quay

Tresemple

Pencalenick
Pond

EXTENSION

Penhale
Mill

ibessow

Tresemple
Pond

St Cohan's
Church
(ruin)

Merther

TRESILLIAN BRIDGE (A390)

Menadews
Farm

Eglosmerther
Manor

Eglosmerther
Farm

nce
m

Tresawson
Farm

St Clement

Penhale
Wood

TRESILLIAN BRIDGE (A390)

TRESILLIAN RIVER

RECOMMENDED WALK

Denas Road
(Permissive path)

Merther Pool

Cregon
Barrow

Private
carriageway to
Tregothnan

PAGE 58

Bar
Meadows

TRESILLIAN RIVER

BLINDMAN'S LANE

Heron
Inn

Malpas

**Merther
Lane**

Fentongollan
Flower Farm

Old ferry
landing
(high water
only)

Malpas
Point

Tregonian
Wood

Fentongollan
Cross

LAMORRAN AND
SETT BRIDGE

ictoria
Point

MOPUS REACH

Tregonian

Kea
Wood

Woodbury
Point

Lambe
Creek
House

Woodbury
Farm

Grimes
Bar

**St Michael
Penkevil**

6

COWLANDS AND COOMBE
WALK (PAGE 48)

PAGE 58

St Clement

St Clement

The little hamlet of St Clement is a good starting point for creekside walks to Tresillian and Malpas. There is a small car park next to the water's edge with enough space for about ten cars. The churchyard has a large carved Celtic menhir (standing stone) called the Ignioc Stone dated to about AD500. It's inscribed partly in Latin and partly in the ancient Irish ogham script and commemorates the death of Ignioc, presumably an important tribal chief. When the Romans left Britain in AD410 it precipitated an extensive migration of Irish to Scotland, Wales and Cornwall. These Irish ogham stones are evidence of the close links between Cornwall and Ireland in Dark Age Britain, something reflected in stories like that of Tristan and Iseult (opposite). Inside the church there is a fine memorial to Admiral Sir Barrington Reynolds (1786–1861) who was born at nearby Penair House. He went to sea aged only ten as servant to his father Captain Robert Reynolds on *HMS Amazon*. He was captured aged eleven during the French Revolutionary Wars after their ship went aground in battle and was wrecked. He and his father were later ransomed and released. During the Napoleonic Wars (1803–1815), his elder brother and his father were killed on active service and he suffered from ill health, which led to him leaving the service. He returned to the Navy in the 1840s after an absence of 30 years and played a major role in the final destruction of the illegal trade in African slaves to Brazil. Reynolds was honoured for this service and retired again to Penair. There are similarly fine memorials to naval officers at St Michael Penkevil Church and St Anthony Church at Place.

Memorial to Admiral Sir Barrington Reynolds

Malpas and the story of Tristan and Iseult

A three-way ferry once operated between Malpas Village, Kea Wood and Malpas Point for agricultural workers. It no longer runs but you might be able to persuade someone at Malpas boatyard to take you. Malpas sits right at the confluence of the Tresillian and Truro rivers, and in poor weather the swollen rivers clash forming large swirling eddies and unpredictable winds sweep along the valleys. This is said to be the origin of its name *Mal-pas* or *bad-passage*. The crossing has long been linked with the medieval tale of Tristan and Iseult. Tristan was the nephew of King Mark of Cornwall whose castle was at Tintagel. He was fighting in Ireland alongside his Celtic cousins against the Vikings, who were ravaging the Irish coast, when he suffered a deep wound in his side and was only saved by the magical healing skill of Iseult, the daughter of Irish chieftain Morholt. When Tristan returned to Cornwall, his uncle became infatuated just by listening to the stories of the beautiful woman and her miraculous healing touch. Calculating that marriage to Iseult would also secure an alliance with the Irish, King Mark sent Tristan back to Ireland with a proposal of marriage. The headstrong Iseult resisted being sent to Cornwall and her father, also wishing to seal an alliance with Mark, asked an Irish witch to mix together a love potion that could be secretly given to Iseult on her wedding night so that marriage and alliance could be consummated. There was a mix-up on the journey back to Cornwall and Iseult took the potion by accident and fell in love with Tristan instead. When the couple reached Cornwall they could not bear to be parted, and ran away just before Iseult was to be married. They were pursued across Cornwall crossing here at Malpas. Iseult was eventually captured and forced to marry King Mark. Tristan only escaped with his life by jumping off a cliff into the sea at Chapel Point near Mevagissey. He fled across the sea and eventually married the daughter of the King of Brittany. He never stopped loving Iseult and soon fell desperately ill again when the wound that Iseult had healed started to bleed once more. A message was sent to Cornwall for Iseult to come and heal him. At first Mark refused, but finally after many months of pleading by Iseult, he let her go. The ship that Tristan sent had orders to hoist a white sail if Iseult was on board but a black sail if they had been unsuccessful. As the ship approached, Tristan asked to be carried to the cliff. Unable to raise himself he asked his wife what colour sail she could see and in a moment of jealousy she told him that the sail was black. Tristan, in despair, died on the cliff. When Iseult arrived she was unable to revive him and threw herself onto the rocks below.

Ferry House on Malpas Point

Parking, shorter walks and leisurely strolls

The ideal way to arrive at **Malpas** is from **Falmouth** or **St Mawes** on the ⑥ seasonal ferry, enjoying the sights and sounds of the river on the way and ending your walk in the **Heron Inn**. *But check your ferry calls and picks up at Malpas*. There is roadside parking in **Malpas** but watch out for traffic wardens – this is a happy hunting ground for them. Don't count on there being free space here in the busy summer months.

St Clement has a small car park right on the water's edge, enough for 7 or 8 cars. There is also parking in the lay-by on the main road (A390) at the end of the path beside **Tresillian Creek**. It's a good level surface all the way.

A walk from Malpas to St Clement and back

*Parking in **Malpas** can be tricky, especially in the summer. As an alternative try the small parking area in **St Clement**. You could also arrive on the ferry from Trelissick, St Mawes or Falmouth but check that it stops at Malpas as, when the tide is up, it goes straight to the quay at Truro without stopping here. In Malpas you can sit out at the **Heron Inn** and look over the river to the heronry in Kea Wood. This walk can be extended along the bank of the **Tresillian River** (blue dotted line). The path is well surfaced so suits bikes and buggies. It's popular with birdwatchers but not particularly spectacular.*

Assuming you arrive by ferry, from the slip at **Malpas**, turn right (with the river to your back) along the road to **Bar Meadows**. About 20m after the turning circle, leave the road on the right as it dips down, then keep left and follow the footpath. You will leave the houses behind and soon cross a stream at the head of **Bar Creek**. The path you will return on (Denas Road) joins here, but to get to **St Clement**, carry straight on up the hill and over the fields.

The return path, called Denas Road (page 38), leaves the back of the small creekside parking area in **St Clement**.

Distance
3.5km (2¼ miles) round trip.
Food and drink
Heron Inn at Malpas. Trennick Mill on the Malpas to Truro Road. Wheel Inn, Tresillian.

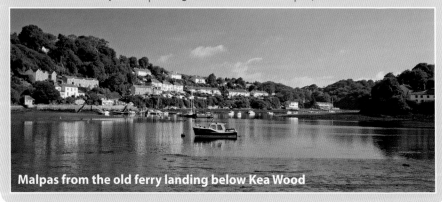

Malpas from the old ferry landing below Kea Wood

Tregothnan, Ruan Creek, Ruan Lanihorne and Philleigh

The Roseland Inn at Philleigh

This deeply rural part of Cornwall is centred around **Tregothnan House** and its wider estate and farms. Most visitors, in their dash to reach St Just and St Mawes, miss this area altogether, but at **Malpas Point**, **Lamorran**, **Sett Bridge** and **Philleigh** there are some of the most memorable places on the whole Fal Estuary. However, there are very few footpaths and very limited access to the riverside, so most exploring will be done by driving around and stopping for short exploratory walks. The oak woods around **Lamorran** are a particularly beautiful sight in the autumn.

Ruan Creek

This last tidal part of the River Fal is called Ruan Creek and, despite its breadth, it very quickly dries out to expose large expanses of mud and shingle as the tide falls. Access to the creekside is very limited and so it is the most undisturbed creek on the estuary and a favourite place for shy wading birds to congregate on the mud flats at low water. There are only two places to get access to Ruan Creek – below Philleigh and around Ruan Lanihorne and Sett Bridge.

Tregothnan House and St Michael Penkevil

Tregothnan is the home to Viscount Falmouth and the Boscawen family. The house is not open to the public, but the large gardens have charity openings in the spring and prearranged groups are able to visit throughout year. The estate produces timber, but also tea, honey and Kea plum jam (page 47). The church at St Michael Penkevil has memorials to Boscawen family members, including a very fine Robert Adam memorial to Admiral Ned Boscawen (overleaf).

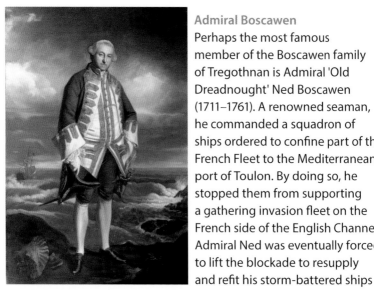

Admiral Boscawen

Perhaps the most famous member of the Boscawen family of Tregothnan is Admiral 'Old Dreadnought' Ned Boscawen (1711–1761). A renowned seaman, he commanded a squadron of ships ordered to confine part of the French Fleet to the Mediterranean port of Toulon. By doing so, he stopped them from supporting a gathering invasion fleet on the French side of the English Channel. Admiral Ned was eventually forced to lift the blockade to resupply and refit his storm-battered ships at Gibraltar. When the French Fleet tried to sneak through the Straits of Gibraltar, he regrouped, setting sail in half-prepared ships, and immediately attacked, scattering and destroying most of the enemy. He finished off the remaining ships in Lagos Bay. This was a violation of the neutrality of Portugal, but never let it be said that international law ever came between a British sailor and his duty to attack a Frenchman. He was famous for his fondness for attacking the French – whatever the odds. One night, a young lieutenant woke him to say that two heavily armed French men-of-war were bearing down on their solitary ship. The lieutenant wanted to know what they should do as they were out-gunned.

"Do!" Ned shouted as he jumped out of bed

"Do! ... We attack of course, it's a Frenchie!" So dressed in his nightgown with his cutlass strapped to his side, he took the helm and fought for the honour of his country. William Pitt said of him, "When I explain my projects to other admirals they always raise difficulties – Boscawen always finds expedients." His fine memorial is in St Michael Penkevil church (right).

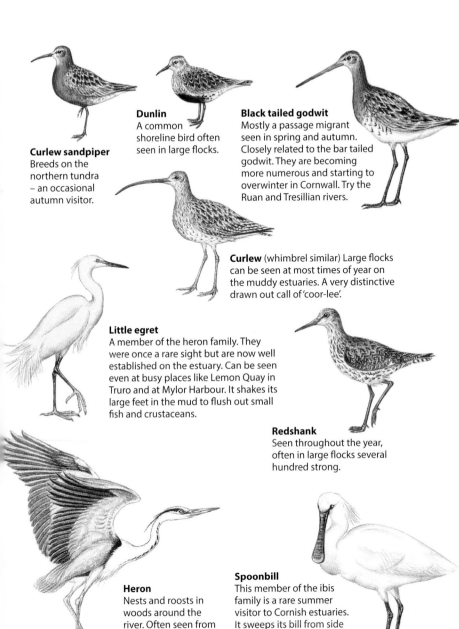

Curlew sandpiper
Breeds on the northern tundra – an occasional autumn visitor.

Dunlin
A common shoreline bird often seen in large flocks.

Black tailed godwit
Mostly a passage migrant seen in spring and autumn. Closely related to the bar tailed godwit. They are becoming more numerous and starting to overwinter in Cornwall. Try the Ruan and Tresillian rivers.

Curlew (whimbrel similar) Large flocks can be seen at most times of year on the muddy estuaries. A very distinctive drawn out call of 'coor-lee'.

Little egret
A member of the heron family. They were once a rare sight but are now well established on the estuary. Can be seen even at busy places like Lemon Quay in Truro and at Mylor Harbour. It shakes its large feet in the mud to flush out small fish and crustaceans.

Redshank
Seen throughout the year, often in large flocks several hundred strong.

Heron
Nests and roosts in woods around the river. Often seen from the King Harry Ferry, in Kea Wood (opposite Malpas) and in Pelyn Creek near Percuil.

Spoonbill
This member of the ibis family is a rare summer visitor to Cornish estuaries. It sweeps its bill from side to side in shallow water to catch small invertebrates. Breeds in southern Europe and North Africa.

Birds of the muddy creeks

The best time to watch is a couple of hours before high water as the incoming tide forces the birds out of the small muddy channels onto the open mudflats. The best places are Hyde's Quay near Ruan Lanihorne, Percuil, Tresillian River and Restronguet.

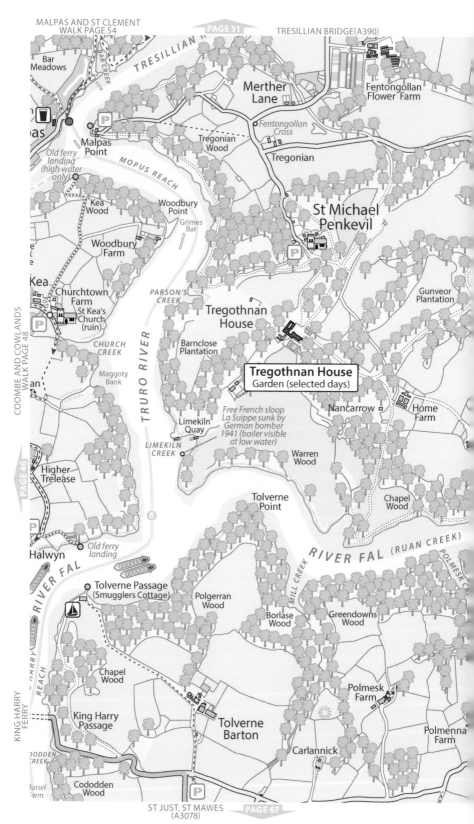

MALPAS AND ST CLEMENT
WALK PAGE 54

PAGE 51

TRESILLIAN BRIDGE(A390)

TRESILLIAN R

Bar
Meadows

Merther
Lane

Fentongollan
Flower Farm

BAR CREEK

Malpas
Point

Old ferry
landing
(high water
only)

Tregonian
Wood

*Fentongollan
Cross*

MOPUS REACH

Tregonian

Kea
Wood

Woodbury
Point

Grimes Bar

St Michael
Penkevil

Woodbury
Farm

COOMBE AND COWLANDS
WALK PAGE 48

Kea

Churchtown
Farm

St Kea's
Church
(ruin)

PARSON'S
CREEK

Tregothnan
House

Gunveor
Plantation

CHURCH
CREEK

Barnclose
Plantation

Tregothnan House
Garden (selected days)

Maggoty
Bank

TRURO RIVER

*Free French sloop
La Suippe sunk by
German bomber
1941 (boiler visible
at low water)*

Nancarrow

Home
Farm

Limekiln
Quay

PAGE 46

Higher
Trelease

LIMEKILN
CREEK

Warren
Wood

Chapel
Wood

6

Tolverne
Point

Halwyn

Old ferry
landing

RIVER FAL (RUAN CREEK)

RIVER FAL

Tolverne Passage
(Smugglers Cottage)

Polgerran
Wood

MILL CREEK

Borlase
Wood

Greendowns
Wood

POLMESK CREEK

KING HARRY REACH

Chapel
Wood

King Harry
Passage

KING HARRY
FERRY

Polmesk
Farm

Tolverne
Barton

Carlannick

Polmenna
Farm

DODDEN
CREEK

Cododden
Wood

Mussel
Farm

ST JUST, ST MAWES
(A3078)

PAGE 67

Tregenna Farm

Gare Farm

STROLL

Trewonnal Farm

Lamorran Wood

RIVER FAL

Ruan Lanihorne

Weir

Sett Bridge

Parson's Hill Wood

P

Lamorran

P

Hyde's Quay

RUAN RIVER

Trethella

Penkevel Wood

LAMORRAN CREEK

RIVER FAL
(RUAN CREEK)

Disused Brick Works

TUCKINGMILL CREEK

Trelonk

kevel

Ardevora Veor

ARDEVORA CREEK

Ardevora Mill

Ardevora

Trenestrall

RUAN HIGH LANES
(A3078)

RECOMMENDED WALK

Polsue Manor

hilleigh

Court Farm

Polglaze Farm

seland Inn

P

Penhallow

Lower Penhallow

White

Sett Bridge

Ruan Lanihorne and Sett Bridge

Crossing the River Fal at Sett Bridge is a lovely way to enter the Roseland. Surprisingly, the bridge is not much more than 100 years old and there was a tidal ford here until the end of the 19th century. The building of the bridge and weir put paid to vessels being able to make it upriver, and the quays at Ruan Lanihorne became the tidal limit on Ruan Creek. This was once a busy little port with a lime kiln, corn mill, blacksmith and quays to bring in coal. The creekside road now crosses the old quays, the original road being the one that arches up and around the church and King's Arms pub. The church is dedicated to St Ruan from Ireland who was converted by St Patrick. We have a few snippets of his life story, for instance his wife accused him of eating their children causing him some problems with his superiors and his flock. He is well known on the Lizard and there's a little more about him in our *Lizard Guidebook*. The tall chimney of Trelonk brickworks (no public access) stands above the trees; it used river silt to make red bricks. Truro Railway Station was constructed using them.

Philleigh

A dozen buildings cluster around the church of St Fili who gives his name to the hamlet. Little of his life story survives today except that he was said to have been a companion of Kea and Ruan who also founded churches on the Fal Estuary. They travelled from Ireland landing in North Devon where Fili is remembered at Buckland Philleigh. There is a popular pub, the Roseland Inn here, and a footpath takes you over fields and down to the River Fal and Ruan Creek.

Low tide on the Ruan Creek below Philleigh

Parking, shorter walks and leisurely strolls

Access to river and paths is very limited in this area. However, there are a couple of roadside parking places at **Malpas Point** where you can wander the short distance to the old ferry landing. Similarly, you can park and wander around at **St Michael Penkevil**, **Ruan Lanihorne** and **Hyde's Quay**. You can also get down to the river at **Tolverne Passage**.

We've shown one stroll on the map (dotted blue line). Leave the public road on the hairpin bend in Lamorran Woods and then after 100m where the track splits keep left up to **Gare Farm** (this part isn't an official footpath). Return on the narrow public road. Beautiful hedges in the spring.

A walk down to Ruan Creek from Philleigh

*This is an easy walk down to the river, just long enough to build up a thirst before retiring back to the **Roseland Inn** for a pint. The little muddy beach at the end of this walk is one of the quietest, most off-the-beaten-track places in this book, and one of the few opportunities to get down to the water on this secluded stretch of the river. It hasn't always been this quiet – for hundreds (and possibly thousands) of years this was the main landing beach for local settlements. The path crosses fields from the church and then dips down to the river in a sunken lane or 'hollow way'. The surface has been eroded away so that the lane is now well below the level of the surrounding land – a sign of great age.*

There's parking for 3 cars on the road opposite the community hall in **Philleigh**. The path is signposted down a driveway to the left of the hall. After about 40m the track splits; walk straight ahead onto the grassy footpath and into some woods. After crossing a muddy stream on some building blocks you'll come to a farm track. Turn right onto the track but then keep left as it almost immediately splits. Follow this muddy farm lane out to the open fields. The lane runs more or less straight for about 550m between hedges. At its end ignore the short dog leg to the right, instead go through the metal farm gate in front of you and then diagonally left and downhill to the gap in the hedge. Keep heading diagonally down to the bottom corner of the next field where, in the woods, you should be able to pick up the sunken lane down to the river. Bring binoculars for bird watching. You can explore the foreshore at low tide.

Distance
2.8km (1¾ miles) round trip.

Food and drink
Roseland Inn at Philleigh, Kings Arms at Ruan Lanihorne.

Tregothnan House

Looking past St Anthony Lighthouse to Falmouth Bay and the Lizard. In the immediate foreground are Army or Anthony Steps. They were constructed to connect St Anthony Battery with Crab Quay and Half Moon Battery on the Falmouth side of Carrick Roads. It's now a favourite spot for fishing.

3. St Mawes and the Roseland Peninsula

A famously beautiful balance between the land and the sea

GLANCE AT ANY MAP AND YOU WILL immediately see how close the Roseland is to being an island, only joined to the rest of Cornwall by a narrow waist between Ruan Lanihorne and Gerrans Bay. And just like many islands, the Roseland has that special trait of being able to change its character in the blink of an eye. One moment you can be walking over rolling fields, the next you suddenly emerge beside a wooded creek or tumble onto a grassy cliff. It's this variety of landscape – its open aspect, its famously beautiful balance between fields, creeks and sea – which makes the Roseland such a popular place to visit.

Most people travelling from Falmouth and Truro arrive on the Roseland by crossing the River Fal on the car ferry at **King Harry Passage**. Crossing here saves a great deal of time compared to the alternative inland route, which refuses to get its feet wet and instead circumvents the whole tidal estuary by arching north of Truro to Tregony, St Just and eventually St Mawes. The boundary of the Roseland is set here by the middle reaches of the River Fal as it passes King Harry Passage and then by **Ruan Creek** as it turns east and continues to the tide's limit at **Ruan Lanihorne** and Sett Bridge (an area covered on page 55). Access to the waterside on Ruan Creek is limited to a single path below Philleigh (the walk described on page 61) and around Sett Bridge and Ruan Lanihorne.

On these shallow upper reaches of the estuary a dense stillness and silence suffuses places like Sett Bridge, and the open sea feels a long way away. That atmosphere soon starts to dissolve as you travel south across the Roseland and instead the scent of the ocean is carried inland on the breeze so that you often smell the sea long before you see it. Such is the influence of the sea that, around **St Mawes**, it's often quicker to jump on a boat than to get around by car.

HIGHLIGHTS

PERCUIL RIVER
A wide choice of beautiful creekside walks.

ST JUST-IN-ROSELAND
Pasco's Boatyard, the Bar and St Just Church.

USEFUL FERRIES

Check the Fal River website for timetables, latest information and updates. Main ferry landing places are marked ● on the maps. Other potential landing places are marked ○.

❹ A year-round foot ferry runs between St Mawes and Prince of Wales Pier (PWP), Falmouth. In the season some services also call at Custom House Quay (CHQ), Falmouth.
❺ A small seasonal foot ferry runs from St Mawes to Place, opening up access to walks around St Anthony and Portscatho.
❻ A seasonal foot ferry runs from St Mawes to Trelissick. You can pick up a ferry to Malpas (low water) and Truro (high water only) from the pontoon.
❼ Seasonal cruises run from St Mawes to the Helford River.
❽ Year-round sea safaris leave from St Mawes for Gull Rock, Falmouth Bay and The Manacles.

Roundhouse at Veryan

A year-round pedestrian ferry runs between Falmouth and St Mawes. A popular path runs alongside Carrick Roads from St Mawes to St Just-in-Roseland, Messack and the D-Day embarkation beach at Turnaware Bar.

In the season a little foot ferry operates between St Mawes and Place. It crosses only a few hundred metres of the Percuil River but saves a round trip of thirteen kilometres by road. Once at **Place Quay** you have a choice of walks, any of which would probably feature in a list of the best in Cornwall. Turn right past St Anthony Church and you are on the way to **St Anthony Head** and Zone Point with their magnificent views over Falmouth Bay. This high up you get a grandstand view of the bay busy with small tankers from Falmouth Docks heading out to refuel ships anchored in the bay and the sight of billowing spinnakers as yachts head for the open sea. If you turn left from Place Quay, the path follows the Percuil River to **Porth Farm** and the family beach at Towan. A little further upriver and the flawless creekside walk around Percuil and Polingey Creek takes you to one of the most beautiful parts of the whole estuary (photo page 81).

On this long, narrow peninsula, the footpaths knit together two different landscapes: that of creek and field in the Percuil River with that of cliff and beach facing onto the open sea at **Gerrans Bay**. Gerrans is just a few hundred metres from the Percuil River at this point, and the focus turns to the coast as the full sweep of Gerrans Bay is revealed at **Portscatho**. This is the land of King Geraint, an 7th century Celtic king and one of the last rulers of Dumnonia, the southwestern kingdom of the Celts. His name is remembered in many place names on the Roseland, which was his home. He is said to be buried in Carne Beacon near Veryan. There's a string of beaches in Gerrans Bay, first at Porthcurnick, then the little coves at Parbean, Creek Stephen and Curgurell and finally the huge beaches at Pendower and Carne. **Nare Head** is the highest point and has views over Falmouth Bay to the Lizard and up the coast to the prominent headland of the Dodman.

King Harry, Turnaware Bar, Messack and St Just-in-Roseland

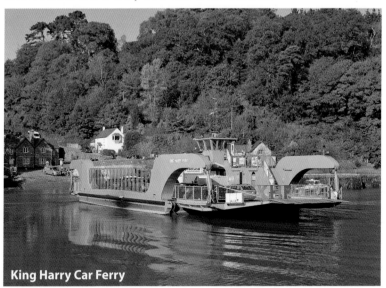

King Harry Car Ferry

The main route into the Roseland from Falmouth and Truro crosses the River Fal at **King Harry Passage**. It's a very enjoyable way to arrive on the Roseland, adding to the sense that you are travelling to a rather special place (which you are). We saw in the previous chapter how accessible the Truro side of the estuary is around Trelissick and Cowlands, but here on the Roseland side, it's much more private. Access for several kilometres either side of King Harry is limited to two solitary paths: one to Tolverne Passage from the public road and one at Philleigh (page 55). That all changes when you reach **Turnaware Bar** and **Messack Point**, and here you are able to walk by the water. By the time you reach **St Just-in-Roseland** you can walk all the way to St Mawes alongside Carrick Roads.

King Harry Ferry

A ferry has plied back and forth at King Harry Passage for at least 500 years – for the past century sedately hauling itself along the thick iron chains anchored between the river banks. There's just enough time as the ferry makes its way across to jump out of your car and take in the views over these middle reaches of the estuary. This part of the River Fal is full of interest, with assorted mussel farm pontoons (the mussels are grown on ropes that hang in the water below), laid-up shipping and seasonal ferries landing at Trelissick pontoon. Crossing the Fal here saves nearly thirty kilometres on the alternative land route that makes its way around the tidal limit of the estuary, crossing the old bridges at Tresillian and Tregony. King Harry can be busy in the summer and you may have to queue on the hill. Have cash ready for the fare.

Looking over to Trelissick from Camerance Wood

Turnaware Bar and Tolcarne Creek

The shingle bar at Turnaware reaches far out into the river pushing the deep channel towards the Trelissick bank (the start of the deep channel is marked by the green buoy). At this pivotal point in the estuary there are greatly contrasting views: to the north, the estuary enters its middle reaches between tall steeply wooded banks; to the south, the view opens out and you can see all the way down Carrick Roads to Black Rock and Falmouth. Like nearby Tolverne, Turnaware Bar was an embarkation point for American soldiers heading to the Normandy beaches on D-Day 1944. The build-up started a year earlier as a wide access road was laid all the way from the main road to the bar with passing places for trucks and tanks and a one-way system that allowed trucks to off-load at the aprons with a return road carved out of the hillside. Load-bearing aprons were constructed on the beach and mooring posts installed for the landing ships (still evident on the foreshore). In the weeks up to D-Day, ever-increasing numbers of troops from US 29th Infantry Division were billeted in tented camps concealed under the tree canopy. The build-up intensified until local woods were teeming with activity. Local people talk of the eerie silence that suddenly descended on the creeks after the convoy set sail on the night of 5th June 1944 bound for Omaha Beach. They had the misfortune to land facing a division of battle-hardened German troops recently transferred from the Russian front. The first wave of landings received 83% casualties in the first three hours. The situation was so dire that the landings on Omaha Beach were nearly abandoned.

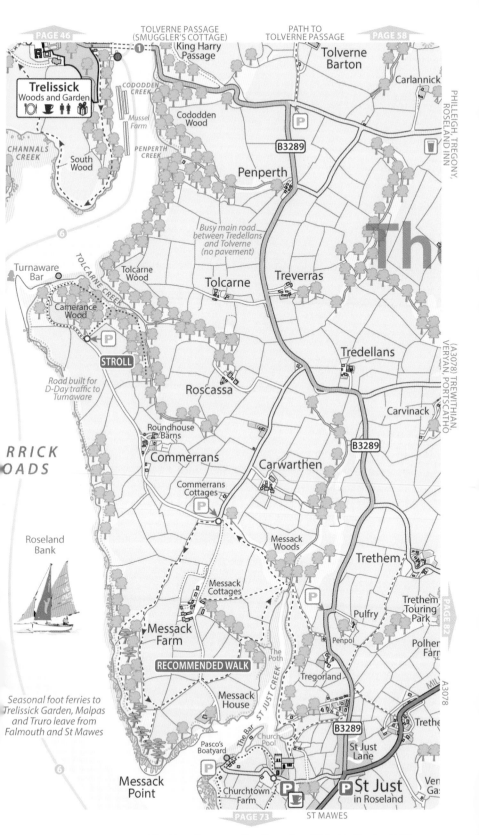

TOLVERNE PASSAGE
(SMUGGLER'S COTTAGE)

PATH TO
TOLVERNE PASSAGE

King Harry
Passage

Tolverne
Barton

Carlannick

Trelissick
Woods and Garden

PHILLEIGH, TREGONY,
ROSELAND INN

CODODDEN
CREEK

Cododden
Wood

Mussel
Farm

Penperth

PENPERTH
CREEK

CHANNALS
CREEK

South
Wood

B3289

6

Busy main road
between Tredellans
and Tolverne
(no pavement)

Th

Turnaware
Bar

TOLCARNE CREEK

Tolcarne
Wood

Tolcarne

Treverras

Tredellans

(A3078) TREWITHIAN,
VERYAN, PORTSCATHO

Camerance
Wood

P

STROLL

Road built for
D-Day traffic to
Turnaware

Roscassa

Carvinack

RRICK
OADS

Roundhouse
Barns

Commerrans

Carwarthen

B3289

Roseland
Bank

Commerrans
Cottages

P

Messack
Woods

Trethem

Messack
Cottages

Trethem
Touring
Park

Pulfry

Messack
Farm

Penpol

Polher
Farm

RECOMMENDED WALK

The
Poth

Tregorland

Trethe

Seasonal foot ferries to
Trelissick Garden, Malpas
and Truro leave from
Falmouth and St Mawes

6

Messack
House

ST JUST CREEK

B3289

MIL

A3078

The Bar

Church
Pool

St Just
Lane

Messack
Point

Pasco's
Boatyard

P

P

Churchtown
Farm

P

P

St Just
in Roseland

Ven
Gas

ST MAWES

St Just Creek

A path runs through the overgrown woods on the southern side of Tolcarne Creek, which children will enjoy exploring. A circular path comes back to the parking area, but you can also follow the stream inland for some way but will eventually have to retrace your steps. Tolcarne Creek was used as a location for the famous 1950 Disney film of *Treasure Island*. I think the shots of Tolcarne (and some taken on the Helford) are the scenes where Long John Silver wades through the shallow water on Treasure Island.

There's a small National Trust parking area at Turnaware Bar. To get there turn off the main road (B3289) where you see the brown sign to Roundhouse Barns (Commerrans and Messack are not signposted from the main road). Drive along the road (laid during World War Two) and past the entrance to Messack and Commerrans farms following the lane past the sign that says 'private road'. The parking area is at the end of the lane. You can walk to Turnaware Bar from St Just-in-Roseland Church following St Just Creek to Messack Wood and then walking up through the fields to join Commerrans Lane.

Messack

The great attraction of Messack Point is the great views across Carrick Roads to Falmouth. Parking is scarce, but it's only a short walk from St Just Church to Messack Wood and from there a circular path runs around the promontory. You can also wander down Commerrans Lane to Turnaware Bar. St Just Creek and the church get late sunshine so it's best visited in the late afternoon or early evening. It's one of the less busy walks, partly because of the slight difficulties of parking.

Messack Wood

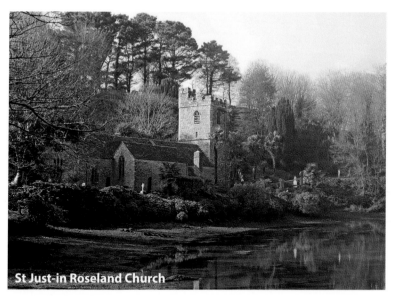
St Just-in Roseland Church

St Just-in-Roseland

In Carrick Roads the deep channel cuts a sinuous path across the estuary between the Roseland and Falmouth banks. Below Messack Point and St Just Creek, it comes in close to the shore before turning back on itself and heading off towards Restronguet Point on the opposite side of the estuary. This bend on the main channel is called St Just Pool and it was used in the 19th century as an anchorage by larger vessels replenishing supplies from the Royal Navy dockyard at Mylor Harbour. It also served as a conveniently isolated spot to quarantine ships arriving with contagions like yellow fever and bubonic plague. Over the centuries there have been several proposals to take advantage of the deep water and to develop quays and docks, but none came to fruition and, as a result, today you have the wonderful timeless combination of waterside church, Pasco's Boatyard and The Bar. On the highest tides, ferries will make a diversion to come into Church Pool behind the Bar to view the church. The churchyard and gardens roll down the hill right to the water's edge making it one of the Roseland's finest beauty spots. Little is known of the life of St Just, although he is said to have been a son or grandson of King Geraint (page 88). The most famous visitor was Joseph of Arimathea, who is said to have arrived here on a Phoenician trading ship to buy tin. He brought with him a young Jesus. There's a public car park, loos and cafe above the church plus additional parking in St Just Lane if needed. In the winter you may be able to park on the roadside right down on the water's edge by Pasco's Boatyard.

The Bar and Church Pool at St Just-in-Roseland

Parking, shorter walks and leisurely strolls

The main parking in this area is above **St Just Church** where you'll also find loos and a cafe. This is a good starting point for longer walks to **St Mawes** or for a stroll around the church and to **Messack Point**. If that's full there's also a car park at **St Just Lane** opposite the turning to the church from the A3078. In the winter you can usually park near the water's edge by Pasco's Yard.

There's a small National Trust parking area at the end of Commerrans Lane for **Turnaware Bar**. Children enjoy exploring the woods and following the stream inland from Tolcarne Creek (it's a dead end so you will need to retrace your steps).

A walk from St Just-in-Roseland Church to Messack Point

This walk is a mix of creek, woods and wide views from Messack Point over Carrick Roads to Falmouth. St Just can be busy in the summer but numbers soon thin out as you walk along St Just Creek.

Park above **St Just Church**. Walk down through the churchyard to the creekside and follow the path past **St Just's Well**, through the woods and fields to the head of **St Just Creek**. Cross on the concrete walkway at the head of the creek below **Messack Woods**. Your return path will arrive here after following the creekside, but for now keep straight on up the hill with the stream and hedge on your right. You will come to Commerrans

Lane. This concrete road was constructed during World War Two to improve access to Turnaware. Step onto the road for just a few metres and the path is signposted just to the side of the entrance to **Messack Farm**. Pass though a small plantation of trees. After about 30m you will emerge in a field. Keep the hedge on your right and go to the corner and through the hedge. After 20m turn right, through the hedge and then immediately left so that the hedge is now on your left. Keep a look out for the path dividing – you have the option of staying high with views or dropping down closer to the water's edge. The paths reunite above **Messack Point** and the single path crosses the track to **Messack House** and rounds **The Poth** to **Messack Wood**. Cross the concrete bridge at the head of **St Just Creek** again and head back to **St Just Church** and your starting point.

Distance
5.9km (3¾ miles) add 3.5km (2 miles) to walk to Turnaware Bar.
Food and drink
Miss V's Tea Hut at St Just-in-Roseland Church, Roseland Inn at Philleigh, Co-op and other shops in St Mawes.

On the highest tides ferries come right into Church Pool at St Just

St Mawes

Summers Beach at St Mawes

St Mawes is the prettiest village on the estuary. It's small enough to walk around in an afternoon but large enough to have all the things you would want for a satisfying visit: a pretty waterfront to wander along, a choice of beaches to suit your mood, a castle to visit, lots of places to eat and fine walks in all directions. A regular year-round passenger ferry connects St Mawes to Falmouth for shops, Pendennis Castle and the National Maritime Museum. Seasonal ferries run to Trelissick Garden and across to Place Quay opening up walks to St Anthony, Towan Beach and Portscatho. And if that's not enough then you can walk up to St Just-in-Roseland and walk by Percuil River, the prettiest creek on the whole estuary. On the way you'll pass the boat yards at Polvarth and Freshwater where they build working boats (like the ones still busy on the oyster fishery), luxury yachts and Cornish pilot gigs, which are raced around the Cornish coast. There's a large car park and visitor information centre in the heart of the village.

St Mawes was an early Christian saint who lived here in a monastic cell sometime in the 5th or 6th century. The only remains are of his holy well, which is tucked behind Victory Steps in St Mawes; it's very modest and easily missed – thousands pass it every year without even noticing. Unlike his near neighbours, St Just and St Anthony, his sanctuary never developed into a parish church, and his chapel fell out of use in the Elizabethan period (1558–1603). Like many Celtic saints, he has a colourful life story. His mother was from Brittany. When her family discovered she was pregnant they cast her adrift in an old barrel. This was where St Mawes was born and where he spent

St Mawes

the first months of his life. They were shepherded by seabirds and fishes as they drifted on the currents and tides, eventually being cast ashore on the coast of Ireland where Mawes grew up. On reaching manhood, he decided to return to his mother's home and passed through Cornwall on his way back to Brittany. He travelled with Budoc, whose church is near Budock Water west of Falmouth and with whom he shares a similar birth story. He is greatly revered in Brittany (as St Maudez) as a famous teacher and healer.

St Mawes Castle

The construction of this small elegant castle was started in 1540 by Henry VIII (1491–1597). It was designed to complement the gun batteries on the Falmouth side of the estuary, to directly defend the important anchorage of St Mawes Harbour and the main shipping channel into Carrick Roads, which passes on the St Mawes side of Black Rock. The cloverleaf layout was based on the latest Italian and German military theory making it one of the first true artillery coastal forts in Britain. The multilevel gun platforms (page 74) were specifically designed to create overlapping arcs of fire for the newer and more powerful guns of the time. Its low-lying position allowed cannon to skim shot across the surface of the water, increasing the range of the guns and striking at a ship's most vulnerable point near the waterline. However, its sea level location left it exposed to attack from above on the landward side, and the only time shots were fired in anger was during the English Civil War (1642–1651), when it was quickly captured by the Parliamentarian Army. This type of coastal battery reached a high point of development in the late 19th century, and there are two fine examples from that time that guard Carrick Roads, one at Half Moon Battery below Pendennis Castle (page 25) and one on St Anthony Head (page 76). There is a large car park and picnic area by St Mawes Castle and it is a good starting point for walks up to St Just Church and the circular walk to Nanshuthall returning by the Percuil River. Castle Beach is a popular sun trap and place for families to picnic, swim and enjoy the views.

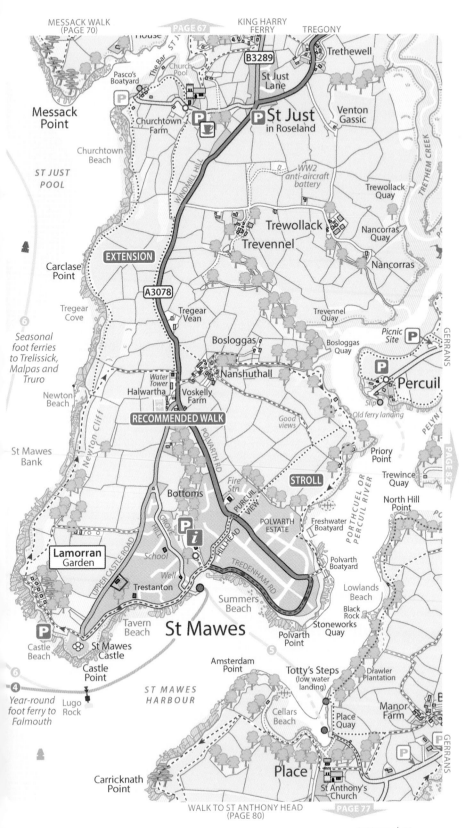

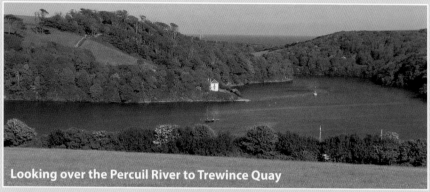

Looking over the Percuil River to Trewince Quay

Parking, shorter walks and leisurely strolls

The main car park in **St Mawes** is right in the centre of the village next to the **Roseland Visitor Centre**. There's also a large car park at **St Mawes Castle**, which is a good starting point for a walk to **St Just-in-Roseland**. In **St Just**, the main car park is above the church, where you'll also find loos and a cafe. This car park is occasionally closed if there is a service. There's also a car park at **St Just Lane** on the main road (A3078) just opposite the turning to the church.

For a short stroll in **St Mawes**, turn up Hillhead, turn right at the main road, then into **Polvarth Estate** and **Percuil View** (photo above). Return along the water's edge.

A walk from St Mawes to Nanshuthall and along the banks of the Percuil River

A popular waterside walk that circles around ***St Mawes****, first following the banks of Carrick Roads, then turning inland to return beside the* ***Percuil River****.*

Park at the main car park in **St Mawes**. Return to the road and turn right following the road past the harbour and above Tavern Beach to **St Mawes Castle**. Leave the public road above the castle and follow the tarmac track (**Castle Drive**) past the car parks and houses. The track ends and a path now takes you on to open fields. Follow the path through a series of increasingly narrow fields. Above **Newton Beach**, leave the waterside path (which heads off to St Just) and look out for a path on the right.

Take this and walk up the hill through two fields towards the prominent water tower on the skyline.

At the main road turn right, and after 50m take the concrete farm track on the left. Just past **Voskelly Barn** and **Nanshuthall Farm** the track splits. Keep left towards **Nanshuthall Cottages** (going straight/right takes you to the good views on the high ground overlooking Trewince – photo above). After **Nanshuthall Cottages** the track snakes around for 200m. Just before **Bosloggas** a path leaves the track on the right. Take it and follow the valley down to the water's edge. Now turn right and follow the well-used path as it passes through fields beside the **Percuil River**, skirting inland around houses. Small access lanes will take you back to the main road at **Freshwater** or **Polvarth** boatyard. Follow the main road as it takes you back to the centre of St Mawes.

Distance
St Mawes–Newton Beach–Nanshuthall –Polvarth 6km (3¾ miles).
Extension to St Just adds 4km (2½ miles).

Refreshments
Lots of choice in St Mawes, Miss V's teas in St Just.

St Mawes Castle

Place, St Anthony Head, Porth Farm and Towan Beach

Place House

This area around **St Anthony Head** is one of the most beautiful parts of Cornwall. As well as sweeping views and riverside walks, there are sandy beaches at **Molunan**, **Porthbeor** and **Towan** and bird colonies and seal caves at **Zone Point**, and all within walking distance of each other. A seasonal foot ferry operates between St Mawes and **Place**.

Place House and St Anthony Church

The name Place seems to come from *palace*, as the existing (mainly Victorian) house stands on the site of a 10th century priory, and this is thought in turn to stand on the site of an older Celtic monastery dedicated to the Celtic saint *Intenyn*. His name was later Latinised to *Anthony* (as it was at St Anthony-in-Meneage on the Helford). Henry VIII and Anne Boleyn are said to have spent part of their honeymoon in the priory. It was Henry's annulment of his first marriage to Catherine of Aragon that led to the fracture with Rome and to dissolution of the monasteries. At Place this became literally true, as Henry is said to have ordered the priory dismantled and the stone reused in the construction of St Mawes Castle. The only part of the priory that survived is St Anthony Church, which, although it has been almost completely rebuilt, retains the early plan and some 12th century stonework around the south door. Inside there are two fine monuments to famous 17th and 18th century members of the Spry family, who then owned Place House. Place once sat at the head of a small inlet that, like Froe and Polingey, was sealed as far back as the 16th century to make a tidal mill pond. It was infilled in 1860 to create the lawn in front of the house. Place House is not open to the public.

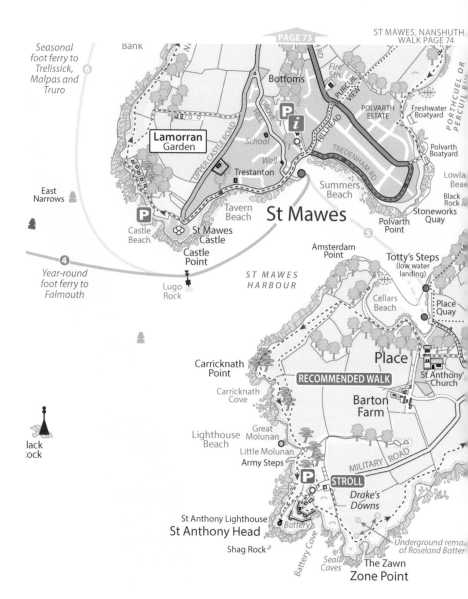

St Anthony Head

St Anthony Head is first thought to have been fortified during the
Napoleonic Wars when a small battery of 24-pounder guns were
installed here. Their purpose was to bolster the defences of St Mawes
Castle in protecting the deep channel into Carrick Roads, which runs
close under the headland at this point. The battery was disbanded
soon after hostilities ended, but as the 19th century progressed, new
instability and revolution in Europe revived fears of invasion. As the
century came to an end, Britain, France, Germany and Russia were
engaged in an arms race, most obviously in the rivalry to develop ever
larger and more powerful naval ships, the so-called dreadnoughts.
There were rapid advances in naval gun technology too. In 1875 ships

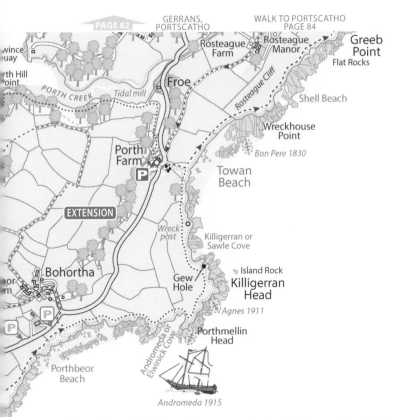

Greeb Point
Flat Rocks
Rosteague Manor
Rosteague Farm
wince uay
rth Hill oint
PORTH CREEK
Tidal mill
Froe
Rosteague Cliff
Shell Beach
Wreckhouse Point
Porth Farm
P
Bon Pere 1830
Towan Beach
EXTENSION
Wreck post
Killigerran or Sawle Cove
Bohortha
Gew Hole
Island Rock
Killigerran Head
Agnes 1911
Porthmellin Head
Andromeda or Elwinick Cove
Porthbeor Beach

Andromeda 1915

were able to fire shells three kilometres, but just 25 years later that had increased to thirteen kilometres. It was obvious that the existing gun batteries defending Carrick Roads were inadequate, so in 1895 work started on much larger defences here and just below Pendennis Castle at Half Moon Battery. Their new six-inch guns were a better match for this developing threat. Personnel moved between the batteries by launch from Army Steps at Little Molunan (page 62) and Crab Quay on the Falmouth side. At the end of World War One the guns were dismantled only to be hastily reinstalled just 20 years later on the outbreak of World War Two, and by December 1939 St Anthony Battery was fully operational again. In 1943 construction of a second battery, the Roseland Battery, was started above Zone Point. This was designed to extend the arc of fire eastwards over Gerrans Bay. Three emplacements were constructed sitting above bombproof magazines. In the end they were never fully armed as the threat of invasion waned once more. The infilled gun pits are still traceable as patches of uncultivated ground in the field above Zone Point. The advent of the atom bomb rendered this sort of coastal battery obsolete, and both St Anthony and Half Moon batteries were decommissioned for good in the 1950s. Instead, Royal Observer Corps nuclear monitoring posts like the one at Nare Head (page 90) were built to spot the detonation of atomic bombs and report back on the levels of radiation fallout.

St Anthony Battery

Half Moon Battery has been refitted with guns, so it now appears much as it did in World War Two (page 25). St Anthony Battery is less complete, but one of the infilled gun pits has been excavated and the National Trust run tours of the ammunition stores and battery buildings in the season. A leaflet giving a more detailed history is available from the car park attendant. The lighthouse below the battery was built in 1834. Look out for cormorants and shags drying their wings on Shag Rock.

Zone Point

Zone Point gets its name from the Cornish word *zawn* for *narrow cleft*, usually in a cliff. It's a common name further west around Land's End (locally it's also sometimes called a *drang*). In this case an obvious narrow inlet leads to a deep cave, one of number on Zone Point that grey seals breed in during the autumn. Fulmars and other gulls nest on the sheer cliff above Battery Cove. They can be watched from the National Trust bird hide in the moat below St Anthony Battery (the building is the command post for the old gun battery above).

Porthbeor Beach and Bohortha

Porthbeor is made up of the Cornish word elements *porth* for *cove* and *beor* or *meur* for *great* or *big*, and it's the Roseland's most dramatically set beach. Cliff falls in recent years have closed the main access from the clifftop and many people now arrive by boat. Porthbeor tends to lose the sun in the late afternoon. There is parking for about ten cars on the road nearby. Bohortha is a sweet little hamlet, very typically Cornish with its collection of farms (*buorth* is Cornish for *cow yard*). It's a good short cut to the Percuil River.

Porthbeor

Towan Beach

Killigerran Head

In Cornish *kelli* means a *grove of trees*, so this place is Gerran's or Geraint's grove. He was a Dark Age king of the Dumnonii, the Celtic tribe of the southwest (page 88), and his name appears in place names across the Roseland. Local folklore says that Geraint built a small isolated cell here where he could pray in peace.

Porth Farm, Towan Beach and Froe Tidal Mill

The National Trust car park and loos at Porth Farm serve the popular family beach at Towan, and you'll usually find an ice cream or mobile tea van here in the summer too. *Towan* is Cornish for *sand dune*, and the beach is one of the best on the Roseland. The soft sand is rich in alkaline shell fragments and has been used for generations to 'sweeten' and improve the fertility of local acidic soils. Porth is also a good starting point for walks on the coast and past the old tidal mill at Froe on the Percuil River. Roseland streams are not strong enough to power conventional water mills so, in the past, the power of the tides was harnessed instead. Froe is the last intact example (photo overleaf), but there were once three on the Percuil River. The one at Polingey is tumbled down now (page 84) and the one in front of Place House was long ago infilled to make a lawn (page 75). The principle of operation is simple – a hefty retaining wall is built across the mouth of a narrow creek and a one-way gate allows the sea to flow in as the tide rises but retains it as the tide falls. At low water, the miller releases the water to turn a wheel and starts milling his corn. In this part of the world even the miller had his life governed by the tides and moon.

Froe tidal mill

Parking, shorter walks and leisurely strolls

This section is neatly topped and tailed by the large National Trust car parks at **Porth Farm** and **St Anthony Head**. You'll also find 5 or 6 roadside parking spaces above **Porthbeor** (the cliff here has suffered a series of falls in recent years and access from the clifftop to Porthbeor Beach has been closed).

For short walks there are any number of combinations from the car parks at St Anthony Head and Porth Farm. The views from **St Anthony Head** are worth the parking fee alone. From here it's also an easy stroll to **Zone Point** or down to the **St Anthony Lighthouse** and **Molunan Beach**. It's an easy stroll from **Porth Farm** to **Towan Beach**.

A walk from St Anthony Head to Zone Point, Porthbeor, Bohortha and Place

*This is one of the best walks on the Roseland. We've started from **St Anthony Head** but you could arrive at **Place Quay** on the seasonal foot ferry from **St Mawes** or make a longer walk by starting from **Porth**.*

Park at the National Trust car park at **St Anthony Head**. Walk past the old officers' quarters and the battery itself. Skirt around the top of Battery Cove to **Zone Point**. Keep a lookout for seals. Follow the coast until you are above **Porthbeor Beach**. Turn inland across the narrow field and onto the public road. Turn right and after 50m, turn left down the little lane to **Bohortha**. The road curves left into the hamlet, then after about 100m, makes a sharp

right. At that point ignore the road and keep straight ahead on the unmade farm track past the little red postbox. Continue for 200m to the end of the farm track. Here the path splits (the right-hand path takes you to Place Quay, the left to **St Anthony Church**). Keep left and cross the field to the public road. Cross the road and follow the path past the church and behind **Place House**.

Follow the track around and above **Cellars Beach** (a pilchard fishery operated from here). About the middle of the beach look for the path as it leaves the track and turns into the field (easily missed). Turn right and keep the hedge on your right. Walk up to the corner of the field. Pass through the hedge. Now you have the option of taking a higher path or, taking the lower path – they meet above **Great Molunan**.

Distance
St Anthony–Porthbeor–Bohortha–Place Church–Molunan 5.2km (3¼ miles). Extension to Porth Farm returning by the Percuil River adds about 4km (2¼ miles).
Refreshments
Portscatho and Gerrans for pubs, cafes and food shops. There's usually a mobile tea van at Porth Farm in the season.

St Anthony Lighthouse and Shag Rock

Portscatho, Gerrans and the Percuil River

Early morning at the National Trust picnic area near Percuil

Although the villages at **Portscatho** and **Gerrans** are now a single settlement, they still retain contrasting outlooks from their original founding. Portscatho looks to the sea and is gathered around the small harbour. Gerrans, on the other hand, congregates around the church at the top of Gerrans Hill and is concerned more with farming and the land. As this is the Roseland, though, the sea is never far away, and the **Percuil River** draws the tide deep into the heart of the farming landscape. The river's course and the coastline run in parallel for several kilometres and are separated only by the width of a few fields so that you can easily move between the two, stitching together longer walks. One note of caution though: avoid, if you can, routes that involve walking on the narrow road between Trewince and Porth, which is often busy with traffic in the summer. On this coast there are two great family beaches at **Towan** and **Porthcurnick** plus lots of more isolated small coves and inlets to visit.

Portscatho and Gerrans

This is one of the best places to be based on the Roseland, less busy than St Mawes but full of life with a working harbour to wander round, cafes, two pubs, a food shop and a gallery. In late August a summer regatta is held on Tatams Beach with swimming and raft races, sand castle competitions, barbecues, music and stalls. At the top of Gerrans Hill stands Gerrans Church, its tall spire specifically raised in the 18th century to provide a navigation daymark for Portscatho fishing boats. There is an interesting small exhibition on Roseland life at the Gerrans Parish Heritage Centre near the church.

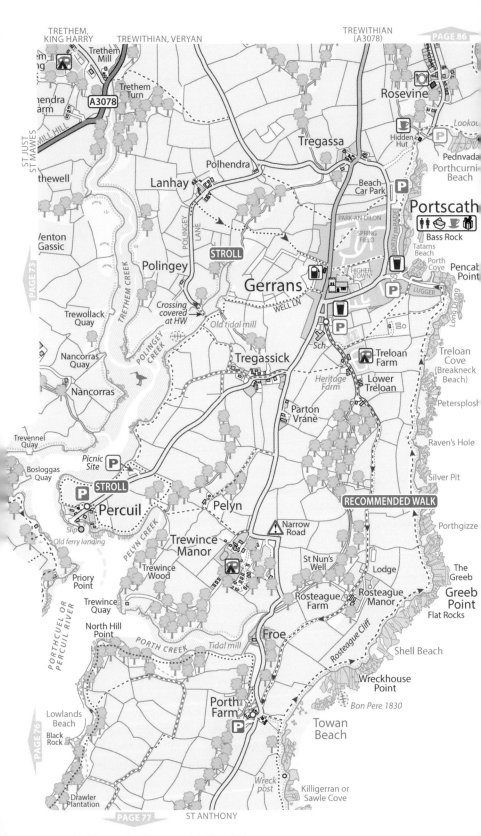

Porthcurnick Beach

Porthcurnick and the Hidden Hut

This is one of the most popular family beaches on the Roseland being sheltered and within easy walking distance of Portscatho. The little beach cafe is called the Hidden Hut and it has feast nights in the season. It's an outdoor family meal gathered around an open fire. You will need to buy a ticket online (numbers are limited) and bring your own plates, cutlery, wine and warm clothing. There is lots of parking in the beach car park plus a little roadside parking at Rosevine (rarely free in the summer).

Percuil River and Polingey Tidal Mill

The Percuil River takes the prize as the most effortlessly beautiful of all the creeks on the Fal Estuary. In the past it has seen a great deal of activity; nearly every farm had its own quay (most of which are somewhat tumbled down but are fun to visit in a kayak) and the river has a long history of oyster fishing, although most commercial activity is now based in the northern half of Carrick Roads. The remains of an old tidal mill are revealed in Polingey Creek as the tide falls (photo overleaf). This was one of a trio of tidal mills on the Percuil River; one still stands at Froe (photo page 80) and one once stood in front of Place House (page 75). The tumbled walls of Polingey Mill make a convenient causeway across the creek to Polingey Lane, which is a beautiful stroll from Gerrans in the early summer. There are large car parks at Gerrans and Percuil. At Percuil the path skirts around the hamlet itself, entering the back of the car park near the loos and leaving the road about ten metres up the hill from the top entrance of the car park where it makes its way to Pelyn Creek. Return to the car park at Percuil through the woods above Pelyn Creek and past the National Trust picnic area. There is a heronry in Trewince Wood.

Porth Farm, Towan Beach and Rosteague

The National Trust car park at Porth is ideal for the popular beach at Towan or as a starting place for longer walks. From here you can walk in almost any direction and find a beautiful walk: to Gerrans and Portscatho (see overleaf) or along the coast and the Percuil River to Place, St Anthony Head and Porthbeor (see previous section).

Portscatho Harbour with Nare Head and the Dodman in the distance

Parking, shorter walks and leisurely strolls

There's a little parking in The Square at **Portscatho** but many more spaces at **Porthcurnick Beach Car Park**. **Gerrans** has a free car park. There's a large National Trust car park at **Porth Farm**, a large car park at **Percuil**, plus a National Trust picnic area on the road just before.

Lots of short walks in this area, but beware walking on the road between Trewince and Porth Farm: it's narrow and busy in the summer. We've shown two strolls (dotted blue line). One leaves behind the loos in **Percuil Car Park** and returns on the road just above the car park entrance. The other, from **Gerrans**, crosses **Polingey Creek** to **Lanhay** over the old tidal mill.

A walk from Gerrans to Porth Farm returning along the coast from Towan Beach to Portscatho

*A mix of cliff and coast with a sprinkling of tiny beaches and coves – ideal places to sit, picnic and pass the time of day. Inland it follows the old road past **Rosteague** to **Towan Beach**. Like many walks on the Roseland, this one is easily extended into a day-long expedition taking in the paths around Percuil or, by walking from the ferry landing at Place Quay to Porth Farm. You have the option of catching the bus back to St Mawes from Gerrans.*

Park at the free car park in **Gerrans** (signposted 200m past the church on Tregassick Road). Return to the public road, turn left and walk down **Treloan Lane** and past the camp site. The road soon becomes a track and follows the spine of high ground past the Elizabethan manor of **Rosteague** (this was the old main road). It joins the current main road at **Porth Farm**. The path to the beach is almost immediately on your left when you reach the road and you might find an ice cream or mobile tea van in the summer. The path to the beach is obvious; then follow the coast back to **Portscatho** heading up Gerrans Hill to the start point.

Distance
6.4km (4 miles)

Refreshments
Plume of Feathers pub in Portscatho, Royal Standard at Gerrans. Portscatho has cafes and a food shop. There's usually an ice cream/mobile tea van at Porth Farm in the summer.

At low tide the remains of Polingey tidal mill form a causeway across Polingey Creek

Gerrans Bay, Veryan, Pendower, Carne and Nare Head

Curgurrell Harbour

It's time to stride out onto the open cliffs on Gerrans Bay. The coastline north of Porthcurnick starts in a low-key way as a series of lovely small coves at **Porthbean**, **Curgurrell Harbour** and **Creek Stephen**. As you approach the wider beaches of **Pendower** and **Carne**, there is a growing sense of momentum as the cliffs climb towards the emphatic climax of **Nare Head** where we end this book.

Dingerein Castle, Creek Stephen and Curgurell Harbour

The ancients had an eye for naturally dramatic settings, so it's no accident that Gerrans Bay is peppered with prehistoric sites. Carne Beacon is the most obvious. Many others now only show up as crop marks or are implied by place and field names – Curgurell, Polcreek and Creek Stephen all contain the Cornish word element *cruc* for *barrow* or *burial mound*. Local stories also tell of treasure buried under the Round House, and this sort of folk memory often relates to an ancient burial mound. Nearby Dingerein Castle is a small prehistoric fort constructed in the later part of the Iron Age (800BC–AD43). Although there is little to see (just a thickened field wall on the main road and part of an oval inner rampart in the field itself), it has a supposed connection to King Geraint (Cornish: *din* or *dinas* for *castle* plus Geraint's name). There's just enough space between the rocks at Curgurrell Harbour to guide a small boat into the tiny slipway. If you look out to sea you'll see buoys marking lobster pots on the reef called The Worla. The catch is usually landed at Portscatho these days but Curgurrell Farm has a great seasonal fish shop. Parking nearby is scarce; we've marked a tiny lay-by on the map where you can stop.

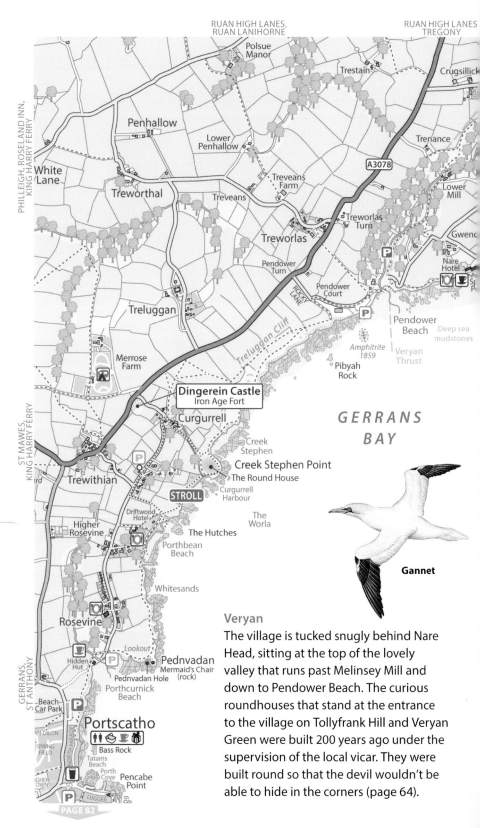

Polsue
Manor

Trestain

Crugsillick

Penhallow

Lower
Penhallow

Trenance

A3078

Lower
Mill

White
Lane

Treworthal

Treveans
Farm

Treveans

Treworlas
Turn

Gwend

Treworlas

Nare
Hotel

Pendower
Turn

Pendower
Court

P

Treluggan

Pendower
Beach

Deep sea
mudstones

Merrose
Farm

Treluggan Cliff

ROCK LANE

P

Amphitrite
1859

Veryan
Thrust

Pibyah
Rock

Dingerein Castle
Iron Age Fort

Curgurrell

GERRANS
BAY

Creek
Stephen

Creek Stephen Point

The Round House

P

Trewithian

Curgurrell
Harbour

STROLL

Driftwood
Hotel

The
Worla

Higher
Rosevine

The Hutches

Porthbean
Beach

Whitesands

Gannet

Veryan

The village is tucked snugly behind Nare
Head, sitting at the top of the lovely
valley that runs past Melinsey Mill and
down to Pendower Beach. The curious
roundhouses that stand at the entrance
to the village on Tollyfrank Hill and Veryan
Green were built 200 years ago under the
supervision of the local vicar. They were
built round so that the devil wouldn't be
able to hide in the corners (page 64).

Rosevine

Lookout

Pednvadan

Hidden
Hut

P

Mermaid's Chair
(rock)

Pednvadan Hole

Porthcurnick
Beach

Beach
Car Park

P

Portscatho

AN DILON

SPRING
FIELD

Bass Rock

Tatams
Beach

Porth
Cove

Pencabe
Point

HIGHER
DOWN

P

LUGGER

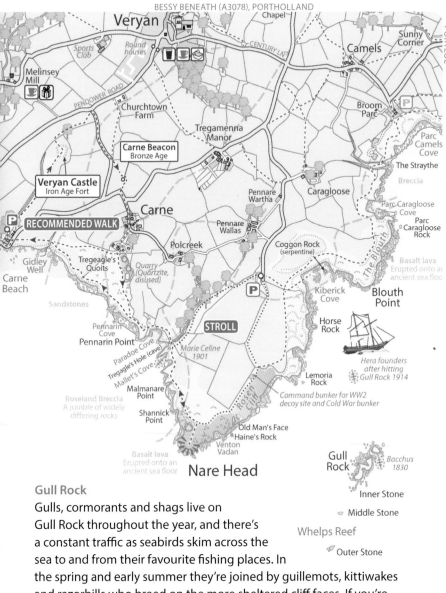

Chapel

Veryan

Camels

Sunny Corner

PORTLOE

Sports Club

Round houses

CENTURY LANE

Melinsey Mill

PENDOWER ROAD

Churchtown Farm

Broom Parc

Parc Camels Cove

Tregamenna Manor

The Straythe

Breccia

Carne Beacon
Bronze Age

Pennare Wartha

Caragloose

Parc Caragloose Cove

Parc Caragloose Rock

Veryan Castle
Iron Age Fort

Carne

Pennare Wallas

Coggon Rock
(serpentine)

Basalt lava
Erupted onto an
ancient sea floor

RECOMMENDED WALK

Polcreek

The Blouth

Gidley Well

Tregeagle's Quoits

Quarry (Quartzite, disused)

Kiberick Cove

Blouth Point

Carne Beach

Sandstones

Horse Rock

Pennarin Cove
Pennarin Point

STROLL

Paradoe Cove

Tregeagle's Hole (cave)

Mallet's Cove

Marie Celine
1901

Lemoria Rock

Hera founders
after hitting
Gull Rock 1914

Roseland Breccia
A jumble of widely
differing rocks

Malmanare Point

Shannick Point

Command bunker for WW2
decoy site and Cold War bunker

Old Man's Face

Haine's Rock

Venton Vadan

Basalt lava
Erupted onto an
ancient sea floor

Nare Head

Gull Rock

Bacchus
1830

Inner Stone

Gull Rock

Gulls, cormorants and shags live on Gull Rock throughout the year, and there's a constant traffic as seabirds skim across the sea to and from their favourite fishing places. In

Middle Stone

Whelps Reef

Outer Stone

the spring and early summer they're joined by guillemots, kittiwakes and razorbills who breed on the more sheltered cliff faces. If you're lucky, you may see the dazzling white shapes of gannets diving into the sea to spear fish. Sea Safari boats from Falmouth and St Mawes come into Gerrans Bay to view Gull Rock and the wildlife.

Pendower and Carne Beaches

These two fine beaches are a popular place to walk at low tide. In the season you'll find ice cream and tea vans at the large National Trust car parks at Pendower and Carne. The Nare Hotel serves teas, lunch and evening meals. There's a small car park on the cliff south of Pendower accessed down Rocky Lane from the A3078 (this is a dead end road). The larger car parks are accessed from the lanes south of Veryan.

King Geraint was carried over Gerrans Bay in a golden boat

King Geraint

Geraint, who gives his name to Gerrans village, church and bay (and to nearby Killigerran Head) was a 7th century Celtic king and saint. He was one of the last rulers of Dumnonia, the southwestern kingdom of the Celts, an area which included modern-day Cornwall, Devon and west Somerset up to the ancient border with the neighbouring Durotriges tribe on the River Parrett. Dumnonia's origins stretch back at least as far as the Iron Age (800BC–AD43), and when the Romans left Britain in AD410, these pre-Roman tribal kingdoms, of which Dumnonia was one, seem to have reasserted themselves. However, they soon came under threat from Vikings and Anglo-Saxons pushing into Britain from the east, and gradually, over the course of the next 500 years, the Celts were pressed back towards the Atlantic. We get glimpses of Geraint in Celtic histories and in West Saxon sources. For instance, in AD705 Aldhelm, scholar and bishop of the early Christian Church in Wessex, wrote to 'King Geruntius . . . the most glorious king wielding the sceptre of the Western Kingdom'. Although his stronghold is said to have been Dingerein Castle just north of Portscatho, it seems more likely that this area was Geraint's home and that political power was wielded from more impressive Dark Age sites in Cornwall like Tintagel or Castle Dore near Fowey. He met his death at the battle of Langport on the River Parrett in Somerset in AD710. The Dumnonii lost and were forced to retreat further west behind the River Ottery that flows through present-day Launceston. A period of stability followed, and the boundary between the Anglo-Saxons to the east and the Celts to the west consolidated so that even today there is a very sharp demarcation line with Cornish place names to the west and English to the east. In AD927, after two centuries of peace, the Anglo-Saxon king Athelstan pushed westward over the Ottery and finally subdued the Celts, sealing victory on the Mayon Rock at Sennen near Land's End.

Carne Beacon – Geraint's tomb

Cornish folklore has Carne Beacon (or the Giant's Chair) as the tomb of King Geraint. His body was laid out at Dingerein Castle and then taken down to Curgurell Harbour to be rowed across Gerrans Bay in a golden boat with silver oars. It miraculously entered the side of Carne Beacon and it's said that he lies there with his golden

Carne Beacon near Veryan

boat. It's a great story but in fact the mound is a great deal older than this legend suggests. Carne Beacon dates from the Bronze Age (2300–800BC) and is one of the largest barrows in Cornwall. It was said to have been even bigger, nearly 90 metres in diameter and 30 metres high, but has suffered from stone robbing. Excavations in the 19th century uncovered a Bronze Age cist (stone lined burial box) containing cremated human remains but no golden boat. The mound had been used for later Bronze Age cremations too and is the centrepiece of a larger Bronze Age cemetery, as two smaller burial mounds are hinted at in aerial photos and a grouping of five other possible mounds, now almost ploughed down, lie in a field next to Carne hamlet. It's quite understandable that a Dark Age king like Geraint would want to be buried here with his ancestors.

Veryan Castle

It's not clear whether this is a large fortified domestic homestead (a round), or a small Iron Age fort like nearby Dingerein Castle. Despite its small size it stands dramatically over the valley that leads down to Carne Beach. Why so much time and effort should be spent creating this earth platform and ramparts in this location is a bit of a puzzle. It seems that the earth ramparts, probably topped with a timber palisade, are less for defence and more for show, designed to impress foreign traders approaching up the valley from below after landing on the beach. It shares this theatrical device with the (admittedly much larger) Iron Age forts at Golden near Grampound and Gear on the Helford. Like both of those sites, it's tucked out of view from the open water (presumably for security) but it reveals itself as you approach from a landing place below. It's certainly nowhere near as imposing when approached from the top of the valley and is not particularly well sited for defence at all. Any attacker could simply stand on the slope above and lob in stones, spears and arrows.

Nare Head and Tregeagle's Quoits

The name *Nare* is a contraction of the Cornish word *pen-nare* for *high promontory*, and at Nare Head you are perched 90 metres above the sea, so high up that it feels like a bird's eye view as you look down on ships in Falmouth Bay. The sea is a beautiful colour from up here, and on sunny days it is a piercing turquoise colour above the sandy bottom and a dark green-brown above the seaweed-covered rocks. There are magnificent views northeast to the Dodman and southwest over Falmouth Bay to the Lizard, and in changeable weather this is a spectacular viewing point as showers race across the bay and shafts of sunlight pierce the clouds.

Standing beside the coast path at Rosen Cliff is a command bunker for a World War Two decoy site (like the one at Nare Point on the Helford). A system of lights set out on the headland was designed to mimic a poorly kept blackout and to draw enemy bombers away from Falmouth. Next to it is an underground Royal Observer Corps nuclear monitoring post from the Cold War (1950s to 1990s), one of hundreds to be used for reporting nuclear bursts and measuring radiation fallout. Both are well preserved and the National Trust run guided tours in the season – search their website for 'Veryan Bunkers'.

The impressive dark cliffs of Nare Head and The Blouth are made up of huge rafts of basalt lava. Readers of our *Lizard Guidebook* may also recognise the milky white rock of Tregeagle's Quoits as quartzite (heavily altered sandstone), last seen in the crags at another Nare Head, north of Porthallow. There are also a few stray boulders of serpentinite, gabbro and schist in Kiberick Cove and in the cliffs to the south. Taken together, this mix of rocks show Nare Head to be part of the same Roseland Breccia that crops out in the Meneage south of the Helford (just across Falmouth Bay). This jumble of rocks is a legacy of a tectonic crash 400 million years ago when an ancient ocean was overridden and destroyed by the northward movement of the continent that forms present-day southern Europe, Africa and South America. As it drove north it acted like a giant bulldozer, scraping and uplifting everything in its path, thrusting great sheets of rock hundreds of metres thick over the younger slates at Pendower Beach, which accounts for the contorted slates there.

Bunker at Nare Head

Pendower and Carne beaches with Nare Head in the background

Parking, shorter walks and leisurely strolls

If you're coming from the Portscatho direction on the A3078, there's a convenient clifftop car park above the southern end of **Pendower Beach** at Rocky Lane. Larger National Trust car parks (with loos) are situated on the northern side of **Pendower Beach** and behind **Carne Beach**. Both are accessed from the minor roads south of Veryan.

Parking for **Nare Head** is in the National Trust car park above **Kiberick Cove** (no parking in Carne). It's an easy walk around Nare Head (dotted blue line on map). The stroll down to **Curgurrell Harbour** from the farm is great. **Treluggan Cliff** is covered with bluebells in May.

A walk from Carne Beach to Veryan Castle, Carne Beacon and Nare Head

*This walk heads inland to take in the prehistoric sites at **Veryan Castle** and **Carne Beacon** and then heads on to **Nare Head** for the views.*

Park at **Carne Beach**. Leave the rear of the car park over a wooden stile and head up the field (keeping the stream on your left) to **Veryan Castle**. From there, continue up, over the stile and keeping the hedge on your right, make for the farm gate and **Pendower Road**. You should be at a T-junction of minor roads. Turn immediately right and down the tiny lane, then up the opposite valley side. As the road starts to curve right, leave it on the corner and walk into the field with **Carne Beacon**, the burial mound of King Geraint. Continue across the field to the road, follow it left to a junction and then down the little dead end road to **Carne Village**. Just after **April Cottage** the lane forks; keep right and just past **The Cottage** the tarmac road becomes a grassy path. Keep left for **Nare Head** (right to return to Carne Beach). Pass **Tregeagle's Quoits** and the old quarry and you'll meet up with the coast path to **Nare Head**. Return along the coast to Carne Beach.

....

Distance
7.1km (4½ miles)

Food and drink
Cafe van at Carne Beach in the season. Meals at the Nare Hotel above Carne Beach, New Inn in Veryan, lunches and tea at Melinsey Mill (not evenings).

Treluggan Cliff

HELPFUL INFORMATION
Getting about

The MV Princessa passing Black Rock and St Anthony Lighthouse on a cruise to the Helford

INFORMATION

For up-to-date information on where to go and what to do go to the **Visit Cornwall** website. It has a good 'What's On' section for local events and festivals. The **Fal River website** is particularly good for ferry, train and bus times (including daily service updates). They print a free **Fal River Area Guide** full of helpful info, timetables and other listings.

Visit Truro Tourist Information Centre
Boscawen Street, Truro.
T: 01872 274555

Fal River Visitor Information Centre
Prince of Wales Pier, Falmouth.
T: 01326 741194

Roseland Visitor Centre
Main car park in St Mawes.
T: 01326 270440

Water Taxi

There is usually a minimum fee, but a water taxi is often good value for groups of 5 or more and means you can get to some of the more remote places on the estuary and coast. For instance, going to Turnaware Bar and then walking back to St Mawes or to Restronguet Point and walking through Feock to Trelissick. Pick up a regular ferry to return. Some possible landing places are marked on the maps like this O. You will need to book in advance.

Ferries

You can get to many parts in this book by ferry in the summer. Buy a **Fal Mussel Card** to get discounts on ferry, train and bus fares.

PARKING

Car parks can fill up quickly in the summer, especially the beaches on sunny days or the attractions on overcast days. At those times, as a general rule, it's best to arrive either early morning or late afternoon if you would like to avoid the crowds. Places like **Pendennis Castle** and **Trelissick** are big enough to comfortably absorb larger numbers of cars and visitors. We've marked the larger car parks like this: P and smaller ones like this: P on the maps (National Trust car parks use a purple colour). There are lots of smaller lay-bys and pull-ins if you know where to look; they usually have space for just a small number of cars. We marked some of them on the detailed maps with this symbol: P. It's quite possible for all of these to be taken in the busy summer months, so be prepared to hunt around for alternatives. Don't be tempted to park in front of farm gates even if they look like they haven't been used for a while. Falmouth has a Park & Ride/Float service to Customs House Quay (CHQ) in the summer. The Maritime Museum is within walking distance of Customs House Quay (CHQ).

Ferry kiosk on Prince of Wales Pier